Praise for **The Que**

This book is a gem – and highly recommended. In *The Question Effect*, Paul McGregor has identified a critical leadership skill not adequately covered elsewhere: asking questions, and the right questions.

Andrew O'Keeffe, author of
The Boss, Hardwired Humans* and *First Leaders

Strategic leaders know that their value lies in the quality of the questions they ask, not the quantity of answers they've memorised. Paul McGregor has captured something important in *The Question Effect* and anyone aiming to lead an organisation or community should take notice if they want to stay relevant in a fast-changing economy.

Alicia McKay, author of *You Don't Need An MBA*

Most leadership books hand you a checklist of answers. The problem is that answers go out of date fast. What Paul does brilliantly is flip the script by giving you the right questions. That's what every leader under pressure *actually* needs.

Leanne Hughes, speaker, consultant,
and author of *The 2-Hour Workshop Blueprint*

In a world that feels increasingly overwhelming, Paul McGregor makes a compelling case for the power of questions. This book shows that clarity doesn't come from having all the answers but from asking bigger and better questions. It's a practical and timely guide for anyone leading in uncertain times.

Matt Church, founder of The Thought Leaders Business School

I work a lot with school leaders who never seem to have enough time. Part of the problem is the expert-at-the-top model of leadership, which puts an impossible load on leaders' shoulders. This book shows a much smarter path, and it couldn't be more timely.

Trudy Graham, AI and Leadership Strategist

The world needs more questions - and this book shows leaders how to ask them. If you've ever found yourself as a bottleneck or close to burning out, this book offers a refreshing way forward. Paul is a trustworthy guide because he's lived this journey - from frustrated leader to global conversation host - and he's distilled what actually makes a difference. Every leader should read this book to understand how to lead by engaging, not by answering.

Becky Hirst, author of *For the Love of Community Engagement*

Having founded, invested in or sold over 100 companies, I've seen how curiosity is the difference between those who make it and those who don't. The founders who win are willing to look wrong on the way to getting it right. Paul makes a compelling case for becoming a master at this throughout the book, utilising real-world experience, his own sometimes-harrowing stories, and some excellent data and case studies. This book is for anybody who aspires to become a better leader, or simply a better partner and listener.

**Josh Comrie, founder of Potentia,
Ambit & Aspire, Host and Author of** *2 Commas*

Paul McGregor is pragmatic and insightful, with a sharp sense of humour. *The Question Effect* is a reflection of those qualities. In a world where leaders are constantly seeking better outcomes, this book offers a powerful toolkit. Paul shows how thoughtful inquiry can drive meaningful change both for the people we lead and the organisations we serve. Highly recommended.

Matthew Needham, author of *Money Talks:
The Leader's Guide to Finance Conversations*

Most leaders think we ask more questions than we actually do. Not only does Paul McGregor make a strong case for curiosity in this book, he offers perceptive questions to ask and credible settings in which to apply them. It's a clearly written resource that takes the pressure off leaders to have all the answers, instead inviting them to "create the space where the best answers can emerge."

**Dr. Rebecca Sutherns, bestselling author of
three books on strategy and adaptability including**
Elastic: Stretch without snapping or snapping back

In a world obsessed with getting the right answer, it's easy to overlook the power of a bigger and better question. The right question, asked at the right time and in the right spirit, can elevate us from dealing with problems to creating new possibilities. In *The Question Effect*, Paul shows us how. Read it and you'll become a more effective leader, a more powerful coach, and a more compassionate contributor to your family, your community, and the world.

Dr Howie Jacobson, author of *The Trigger-Proof Leader*

Great leaders ask great questions - and this book shows you how. There is a lot of brain science around the power of questions to open up people's brains to new possibilities. What I love about Paul's book is that it provides clear questions that leaders need to ask if they want to be effective and have real impact. Highly recommended.

Danette Fenton-Menzies, author of *The Adaptable Leader* and host of the Adapt with Danette F-M Podcast

Paul McGregor is a deep thinker with the rare ability to ask powerful questions. As someone who finds it easier to tell people what to do, I know firsthand how challenging it is to ask questions that shift hearts, minds, and behaviour. *The Question Effect* is the perfect guidebook for building that muscle and learning to lead with curiosity for less stress and more impact.

Colin Bass, Director, Business Lab

Most organisations are designed to reward unquestioning subservience to authority, but progressive leaders understand that their leadership must change. A crucial step involves becoming less of a Knower who prescribes and directs, and more of a Learner who inquires, guides and supports. Using his impressive depth of consultancy experience within all kinds of organisations, Paul McGregor candidly and entertainingly raises readers' awareness of their leadership practices and provides thoughtful guidelines for making changes that matter.

Tom Watkins, author of *Collaborative Dialogue: Self-Management Practices at the Heart of Collaboration*

As Paul explains so well, true leadership isn't about having all the answers, rather it's about having the courage and curiosity to ask better questions. Paul's questions challenge the old model and invite a new one based on shaping the future together. In my mind, that's what *The Question Effect* is about: leadership as an act of shared agency.

Hester Spiegel, Founding Partner, Epic Angels and author of *Thinking Big and Small: A guide to activating your entrepreneurial mindset*

Paul doesn't just talk the talk; he walks the walk. He is a living, breathing example of *The Question Effect*. As someone who has sat on the other side of his questions, I know how much power is in these pages.

Kerri Price, founder of The Facilitators' Network

THE
QUESTION
EFFECT

LEAD WITH CURIOSITY
FOR LESS STRESS
AND MORE IMPACT

PAUL MCGREGOR

First published in 2025 by Hambone Publishing
www.hambonepublishing.com.au

Editing by Mish Phillips, Lexi Wight and Emily Stephenson
Cover design by Hambone Publishing
Interior design by David W. Edelstein

For information about this title, contact:
Paul McGregor
paul@paulmcgregor.co.nz

ISBN 978-1-922357-95-3 (paperback)
ISBN 978-1-922357-96-0 (ebook)

Contents

PART 3: SETTING THE STAGE FOR QUESTIONS

Preface

Have you ever been asked a question so powerful it changed your life?

The first time I clocked this was early in my career, while working in a toxic workplace. One day, I sat down with a mentor and unleashed a litany of complaints about the petty politics and simmering tensions.

He listened and nodded, drawing the full story out of me with patient questions. Then, after an awkwardly long pause, he said: "It sounds like you have a lesson to learn here... Do you want to learn it now or in the next role where you face this?"

I was floored. In 11 seconds, he had cut through months of angst, turning my victim mentality into something else: an opportunity disguised as a problem. He had turned the lights on in a room where I'd been fumbling in the dark!

In the decade since, I've discovered that the right question at the right moment can shift individuals, teams, and even entire organisations. Time and again, I've found that the most effective leaders aren't those with all the answers; they're those who know which questions to ask and how to listen to what emerges.

This is what I call The Question Effect. It's the impact that the right question can have on how people think, feel, and behave. Just like The Butterfly Effect, where a small movement of air can lead to a storm, so too can The Question Effect have an impact long after the words have been spoken.

My journey to this realisation wasn't straightforward.

It began in corporate law where I saw more breakdowns and blow-ups than in any courtroom drama. It was a crash course in dysfunctional leadership.

I watched partners shuttle tearful colleagues into private offices after brutal court sessions, only for them to emerge minutes later, composure forcibly restored, as if nothing had happened. I saw a managing director scream at an intern for making tea during a 70-hour work week. My flatmate, employed at another prestigious firm, once worked two days without sleep after receiving an email from a partner that declared: "There are 20 non-sleeping hours in a day. Get it done!"

These experiences left me floundering and questioning my chosen career path. I couldn't stand the wasted potential. Years of investment in recruitment and training burned because leaders didn't take the time to ask simple questions like: What's getting in your way? What do you need? How can I help?

After waving goodbye to the law, I discovered the same issues as a policy advisor at the Ministry of Justice. Less than ten percent of staff were 'engaged' according to yearly surveys. The atmosphere was thick with resignation and cynicism. We even spent an hour-long meeting arguing over whether we were cynical or sceptical — as if the distinction mattered.

These frustrations drove me to hunt for better approaches to leadership, culture, and engagement. This search took me through leadership roles in non-profits and corporate consulting, working with clients in all sorts of sectors and countries, always looking for what would make the biggest difference in how people work together. I started the *Beyond Consultation Podcast* as an excuse to speak with leaders who were pioneering more collaborative approaches to change, and was shocked when it reached the top 10 in its category.

The best leaders don't always have the right answers, but they always have the right questions.

Through all these experiences, I met countless leaders facing similar struggles, regardless of their industry, country, or organisation. This book is for them. And it might be for you too, if you've ever thought:

- You're the only leader who's making stuff up as you go along,
- You're responsible for everything (but not in control of anything),
- You've become a bottleneck, a bulldozer, or just... really, really tired.

My hope is these pages offer you both insight and relief. The Question Effect provides a much lighter way to lead by reducing the pressure to be the hero with all the answers.

In the chapters ahead, you'll discover how to create The Question Effect, using curiosity and powerful questions to improve engagement, build trust and – ultimately – create change that sticks. At the heart of it is this simple idea: the best leaders don't always have the right answers, but they always have the right questions.

Part 1

THE
QUESTION
EFFECT

CHAPTER 1

A fundamental shift

Sage on the stage or guide on the side

"To ask the right question is already half the solution to a problem."

– Carl Jung

"This is ridiculous," the man shouted from the back of the town hall. "Why did you gather us here to simply tell us what you've already decided?"

I watched as the carefully orchestrated meeting about our dying town centre descended into chaos. The council officers and their consultant stood frozen at the front, their 42-slide PowerPoint presentation only halfway complete.

Just thirty minutes earlier, the mood had been different. Business owners, interested residents, and local officials had filed in, cautiously optimistic about addressing the slow decline of our business district. The same scenario was playing out in communities around the world, with big malls pulling people to the outskirts, online retailers undercutting local shops, and the post-COVID economic pressures delivering what felt like the final blow.

What he failed to do was ask a single question.

The council had invested significant resources to bring in an acclaimed urban planning consultant. His presentation was meticulously researched and detailed. He spoke with confidence about foot traffic patterns, retail psychology, and international best practices.

What he failed to do was ask a single question.

I left that meeting hearing disappointment and resentment from both sides. What fascinated me was both groups wanted the same outcome: a revitalised town centre. Yet they were now further apart than before the meeting began.

I've seen a similar dynamic unfold in hundreds of board

meetings and team standups, client pitches and leadership offsites. Leaders who arrive with nothing but answers create resistance, no matter how polished their pitch or sound their argument. Leaders who arrive with answers *and* thoughtful questions create engagement, even around difficult topics.

The challenge for busy leaders

Much of today's conventional wisdom about leadership keeps getting it wrong. We're told that great leaders are visionaries who inspire us with their charisma and expertise; that they stand confidently at the front, pointing to the horizon, declaring, "Follow me!" And yes, that's part of our role as leaders, but only part of it.

The pace of change facing us as leaders today — from climate adaptation to technological disruption to decaying infrastructure — is too intense for any of us to solve or figure out on our own. Artificial intelligence is transforming entire industries overnight, while geopolitical shifts are reworking supply chains and partnerships that took decades to build. Unlike previous technological revolutions that unfolded over generations, these changes are happening within single budget cycles, making traditional top-down leadership inadequate.

> It's so easy to fill the space with what we know, but there's often more power in creating space for what others might contribute.

But it's hard to see this in all the busyness. And make no mistake, we're busier and more distracted than ever before. The technology that was meant to free us has done the opposite. One third of our days is lost to breaks, interruptions, and searching for information. Another third disappears in meetings and emails. We're only left with an hour or two for focused work.

Leading with answers can work well when things are simple or urgent.

Is it any wonder, then, that many of us lean towards a directive style of leadership? When we're busy, it seems like the faster option to just jump in and sort things out. It's so easy to fill the space with what we know, but there's often more power in creating space for what others might contribute. It may seem slower to begin with, but it's faster in the long run.

Leading with answers or questions

What we're exploring here is the difference between leading with answers and leading with questions. Here's how the two approaches compare:

	Leading with Answers	Leading with Questions
	"Sage on the stage"	**"Guide on the side"**
Involves	Presenting, talking at, giving instructions, setting direction	Engaging, talking with, setting boundaries, asking questions
Suits	Simple or chaotic situations	Complex situations
Invites	Critique	Curiosity
Seeks	Consent	Contribution
Focuses on	What you know	What they know

This book is about leading with questions, but that doesn't mean we should never lead with answers. Sometimes, a direct approach is exactly what's needed, like in an emergency or when we're delegating a straightforward task.

This isn't about abandoning our expertise or avoiding decisions. Nor is it about giving away all our control or authority. It's about knowing when each approach works best. Leading with answers can work well when things are simple or urgent. But most of the challenges we face at work aren't simple; they're complex, messy, and involve lots of people and perspectives — like our town hall meeting at the start of this chapter.

In those situations, our job as a leader isn't to have all the answers but to create the space where the best answers can emerge. That's where The Question Effect comes into play.

How this book works

In Part 1, we'll explore why The Question Effect matters. My aim is to inspire you to adopt an attitude of curiosity in everything you do as a leader. You'll discover the surprising science of curiosity and why it's a universal superpower for leaders.

In Part 2, we'll unpack seven Leading Questions for some of the most common leadership challenges — from vision, to culture, to conflict, and more. The Leading Questions I refer to are not the manipulative kind I learned in law school to trap witnesses, but starting points that invite us into deeper conversations.

Finally, in Part 3, we'll tackle the practical aspects of The Question Effect. You'll learn about the importance of framing and sensing — two critical skillsets that most of us never get taught, but which influence whether our questions are met with an open mind or a closed door.

By the end of the book, you'll understand The Question

Effect and how to put it into action to build trust, improve engagement, and make change that sticks.

We live in a world that desperately needs better questions, and in the next chapter, we'll explore this one: "What's the real cost of ignoring The Question Effect?"

Curious Questions: Set 1

Throughout the book, I'll invite you to consider various reflective questions. I know it's tempting to skip past these, but they will help you apply what we're talking about. You can download a printable workbook for these at paulmcgregor.co.nz/question-effect-toolkit

- How committed are you to reflecting on these questions as you read the book?
- Who or what has shaped your ideas about what leadership means?
- When or where does the pressure to have the answers come up strongly for you?

Experiential Activity 1: Hold and Release

You'll also find short experiential activities dotted throughout the book. I've designed these so you can viscerally experience what we're talking about — without having to leave the comfort of your reading location.

For this first one, let's experience the difference between leading with questions and leading with answers.

Make a fist and squeeze it tight. Hold it and count to ten. Can you feel the tension building?

Now, open your hand. Notice the relief that comes with the release. That's what we're aiming to do with The Question Effect.

CHAPTER 2

Complexity
demands curiosity

The disengagement crisis

"It doesn't make sense to hire smart people and tell them what to do; we hire smart people so they can tell us what to do."

– Steve Jobs

E arly in my consulting career, a client invited me to deliver a training workshop at their strategy retreat. Every single staff member had dressed up and settled in with coffees and lanyards — ready, they thought, to shape the future of their organisation. Sixty people sat in the beachfront venue, with a boat trip planned for the following day. No expense had been spared.

After a brief welcome, the Chief Executive stood to unveil the organisation's new strategy. He spoke confidently for ten minutes, sharing elegant diagrams while explaining the vision that would guide their next three years.

As he wrapped up, he surveyed the room and asked, "Does anybody have any questions?"

After a brief silence, one of the General Managers piped up. "Well, I'd just like to add something," she began — and that's when things started to go sideways. She spoke for several minutes before the other two General Managers, seemingly not wanting to be outdone, took turns adding their own commentary. I fought the urge to check my watch as the 'question time' turned into this executive monologue.

I fought the urge to check my watch as the 'question time' turned into this executive monologue.

Afterwards, we moved to an embarrassing team-building exercise where small groups had to devise a skit using random objects in a paper bag.

I couldn't believe it. They'd gathered all sixty staff, presented a strategy that would affect everyone's work for years to come, and not a single person outside the executive team had said a word. Surely there would be a session later to go a bit deeper? But no. That was it. The strategy had been 'communicated'.

Later, during lunch, I quietly asked a few staff members what they thought about the morning's session and whether they had any unanswered questions.

"I don't really see how it changes anything," one confessed.

"I had questions, but it didn't seem like the right time," another said.

In short, they all had valuable contributions that might have strengthened the strategy or its implementation, but the leadership team never created the space to hear any of it. The Question Effect was absent.

> But something keeps enticing us to take up space with what we already know, rather than creating space for what we don't yet know.

This experience has stuck with me over the years as I've coached dozens of leaders and facilitated big conversations with a wide range of industries and communities. Sadly, I've seen this pattern repeat itself again and again. It's not because leaders are deliberately shutting people down. Most are committed to getting the best out of their people. But something keeps enticing us to take up space with what we already know, rather than creating space for what we don't yet know. But why? What's going on?

It's happened so often — in boardrooms and community halls, in parliaments and at parties — that I've sometimes wondered if I'm the odd one out. Am I the only one bothered by this? Does it really matter if nobody knows about The Question Effect?

A world in rapid transition

What makes this engagement crisis especially troubling is it's happening at precisely the moment we need all hands-on deck. We're facing a ridiculous period of unprecedented transition.

As investor and technology analyst Azeem Azhar recently told his portfolio companies:

> *"The game is changing fast. The global order is being rene-gotiated in real time, driven by the inversion of globalisation and the rise of AI. These forces are creating confusion, hesitation and for the sharpest operators — opportunity."*

Each of these forces would be disruptive on its own. Together, they're overwhelming.

The traditional leadership approach — where the person at the top had the answers — might have worked in a more predictable, slower-moving world. Now it's just a recipe for disengagement and missed opportunities.

The cliché of complexity

These days, I find myself rolling my eyes when I read phrases like, "In today's fast-paced world..." or "With the increasing pace of change and disruption..." — and yet I catch myself saying them too! (They've become clichés for a reason.)

The truth is not every problem is created equal. Some are simple, some are complicated, and some are genuinely complex. I'm not going to overwhelm you with complexity science here, but knowing the difference helps explain why curiosity matters more than ever.

If you talk to complexity geeks, they'll disagree on how to

define it, but I've found the most useful way is to look at the relationship between cause and effect:

- Simple problems have clear cause and effect. If you follow the steps, you get the result. Think making a cup of tea or running payroll. You could do these a million times and get the same outcome: a good cuppa and money in bank accounts.

- Complicated problems also have cause and effect, but it's much harder to see. These problems require expertise and analysis. With enough planning and technical know-how, they can be solved. Think designing a bridge or coding a piece of software.

- Complex problems are different. Cause and effect are unclear because there are too many interconnected parts. Often the nature of the problem changes *while* we're working on it — or even *because* we're working on it. People, relationships, culture, big ideas, global trends and so many other variables are at play. They interact in unpredictable ways. Think leading a team, hosting a meeting, or launching a new product or service into a new market.

As leaders, more and more of our work involves complex problems. Partly that's because it's easier than ever to automate or delegate the simple and even the complicated stuff. And partly it's because fewer problems can be "solved" by a neat plan or a single expert. After all — and here come the clichés — the world is changing faster than ever (I'm so sorry), our systems are globally connected (boring but true), and our workplaces are more culturally diverse thanks to international travel and cheaper technology (I really am sorry).

That's why curiosity — asking more and telling less — is so critical. It's the only way to discover what's changing and adapt in real time.

The hidden costs of disengagement

Imagine you're out with five friends having a drink on a Friday evening. You lift your glass and ask a deceptively simple question, "How's work?"

Look around the table and watch the transformation. Five faces, five completely different reactions — it's like you've pressed five different emotional buttons all at once.

Your friend Adelle's eyes light up immediately, "It's really good right now. We're working on this new project," she begins. And then she's away — launching into work stories

You lift your glass and ask a deceptively simple question, "How's work?"

with the enthusiasm of someone describing their favourite hobby, not their job. When she talks about obstacles, it's with a glint in her eye — as if each problem is just an interesting puzzle waiting to be solved. Adelle belongs to the rare breed: an 'engaged employee'.

Directly across from her, watch as Dave's expression darkens like he's just been served a warm beer. Over his shoulder, you spot a job search app. He's perfected the skill of discreetly scrolling job ads during meetings. He's a 'Loud Quitter'. They physically show up at work, but they're emotionally absent.

Then there's the other three — Craig, Christian, and Carla

— who respond with variations of "It's fine" and a noncommittal shrug. They're clock watchers who leave work on the dot with military precision. Crisis at 4:55pm? Yeah, sorry, that's tomorrow's problem. These 'Quiet Quitters' are doing a good job, but it's not lighting them up. Work is a bland appetiser they endure to afford the main course of life: weekends, holidays, and hobbies they *actually* care about.

> If 80% are disengaged, imagine the untapped energy, creativity, and commitment waiting to be released.

This imaginary pub scene is a living bar graph of Gallup's workplace engagement research, which has surveyed over 35 million employees globally. Their data consistently shows this distribution:

- roughly 20% of employees are engaged (our enthusiastic friend Adelle),
- 60% are disengaged (the three shrugging "it's fine"), and
- 20% are actively disengaged (Dave and his job search app).

When I first encountered these statistics at the Ministry of Justice many years ago, I found them deeply depressing. Four out of five people are disengaged? What a colossal waste of human potential.

But there's another way to view these numbers too. If 80% are disengaged, imagine the untapped energy, creativity, and commitment waiting to be released. Imagine what could become possible if we unlocked that potential.

Of course, disengagement isn't just hard on employees; it takes a toll on leaders too.

Last year, I spoke with a chief executive after his first big team offsite in the new role. "I've never spoken so much in one day," he said, slumping into his chair. "It was overwhelming."

That's the hidden cost of directive leadership. When we feel we must carry all the answers and drive every conversation, it exhausts us just as much as it disengages everybody else.

So, what's driving this pattern of leading with answers? If it's not serving us, why does it persist? It turns out, the root cause is a well-intentioned habit that starts long before we start working.

The high cost of low curiosity

Have you ever issued a direction to staff and then found people resisting, even though you're pretty sure they think it's a good idea? You might have been triggering the same psychological reaction that parents know all too well.

It's like when you were a teenager – moments away from starting to do a chore – and then your parent demanded you do it. What was your instinctive reaction? If you're like most people, you felt an immediate surge of resistance. "I was going to, but now I don't want to!" is the classic teenage response.

> When someone tells us what to do, we instinctively push back to reassert our freedom.

This reaction isn't limited to adolescents. We all experience it. Psychologist Jack Brehm labelled this 'reactance' — the uncomfortable feeling we get when our sense of autonomy is threatened. When someone tells us what to do, we instinctively push back to reassert our freedom.

But so what? What are the costs of this low-curiosity approach? Here are just a few impacts you might have experienced.

Innovation suffers. When leaders have all the answers, team members stop offering ideas. Why would they bother to share their creative solution when their boss already 'knows' what to do?

Blind spots. If we fail to create space for debate, we miss crucial information. How many strategy missteps or poor decisions could have been avoided by hearing from affected people?

> The pressure to have all the answers is a shortcut to burnout.

Talent walks away. People who don't feel heard eventually leave. In fact, feeling that "my opinions count at work" is one of the strongest predictors of employee retention, according to Gallup's engagement survey results.

Problems recur. When we solve problems *for* people rather than *with* them, those problems keep coming back. People never have the chance to develop the skills to address issues on their own.

Burnout. The most insidious cost, though, is to us as leaders. The pressure to have all the answers is exhausting and unsustainable. It's a shortcut to burnout.

I remember coaching a newly promoted director who was working 70-hour weeks and still feeling like she wasn't keeping up. "I don't think I'm cut out for this," she confided. When we examined her calendar, we discovered she was spending over 20 hours every week in one-on-one meetings where team members brought her problems to solve. She had become the organisational bottleneck because she had attached her value to being the solution holder.

The Question Effect at scale

If taking up space with answers creates disengagement, what happens when leaders create space through questions?

Consider how Toyota has used The Question Effect with their employee suggestion system. Since 1951, employees have submitted over 50 million ideas, with approximately 70% being implemented. These range from minor process improvements to significant innovations like a swivelling seat that prevents back strain for assembly workers.

Of course, asking for suggestions isn't enough on its own. I remember seeing a tatty suggestion box in the kitchen at the Ministry of Justice. In my three years there, I never saw anybody put a suggestion in the box, never heard about a suggestion that had been implemented, and never heard a leader encourage us to use the box. It was a gesture, nothing more.

The difference with Toyota is they've put weight behind the system. They've got a process for evaluating ideas quickly, with money and resources to properly test promising suggestions — and put the most successful ones into action.

Of course, questions aren't magic and they need to be genuine. When we ask for input but have already decided the outcome, people quickly sense our insincerity. Similarly, questions that put people on the spot or feel like tests only create resentment.

The Question Effect combines thoughtful questions with appropriate direction — creating space where needed while providing clarity where required. This balanced leadership isn't about abandoning our expertise or authority; it's about deploying them more strategically.

A different way forward

Let's return to that strategy retreat by the ocean. What might have happened if the leaders had approached it with The Question Effect in mind?

Imagine if, after presenting the high-level direction, the Chief Executive had said, "We've outlined the broad direction, but we need your insights to make this work in practice. Let's break into groups to discuss three questions: What excites you about this direction? What concerns do you have? And what would make this work well in your area?"

The energy in the room would have shifted immediately. Instead of passive recipients, staff would have become active contributors. Their collective experience — representing hundreds of years of insider knowledge — would have identified potential pitfalls and improvements. More importantly, they would have left feeling ownership of the strategy rather than merely compliance with it.

Yes, it would have taken more time. There's always a tension between efficiency and engagement. And yes, it might have been messier and less controlled. But the time invested upfront would likely have saved countless hours addressing confusion and cynicism later.

Now, you might be thinking: "That's great Paul, but if The Question Effect was so compelling, wouldn't everybody be doing it?"

In truth, there's something else that's holding us back from embracing curiosity in leadership. The answers lie in understanding the barriers to curiosity itself, along with the leadership lessons from my three-year-old son.

Curious Questions: Set 2

Let's take a moment to let these ideas sink in:

- Where is your work most complex? What makes it so?
- How do you usually respond when things feel messy, uncertain, or overwhelming?
- How engaged do you feel in your work right now?

Remember, you can download a printable workbook for these at paulmcgregor.co.nz/question-effect-toolkit

CHAPTER 3

The question cliff

The power of curiosity

"The world is changing too fast to rely on answers from the past."

– Warren Berger

Conversations with my three-year-old son often go like this:

"Da-aaaa-aad... what's this called about?" he asks as I'm digging in the freezer one morning.

"That's zucchini."

"Why?"

"Uhh, it was going off, so I froze it."

"Why Dad?"

"I've heard it's good in smoothies."

A pause, "Why?"

"Apparently it makes them creamy."

Another pause, another, "Why?"

"I don't know. Can you pass me that glass?"

Fascinating chats, right? But you can see the pattern. He's a typical three-year-old learning and progressing at a rapid pace.

In the book *A More Beautiful Question*, Warren Berger suggests that we ask an average of 40,000 questions between the ages of two and five. Sometimes it feels like my son intends to double that number.

However, the number of questions we ask plummets from childhood onwards. Many adults ask few to no questions in daily life.

The number of questions we ask plummets from childhood onwards.

In this chapter, we'll explore why this happens, and why it matters — as well as the critical role curiosity plays in making our work less stressful and more impactful.

Experiential Activity 3A: The Question Cliff

Imagine a five-year-old asking "Why?" again and again while playing. What judgments do you have about them?

Now imagine a 50-year-old asking "Why?" again and again in a meeting. What judgments do you have about them?

How do your two sets of judgments differ — if at all?

What creates the question cliff?

The decline stems from multiple factors. Yes, adults naturally know more than children, but our education system accidentally dampens our tendency for questions as well.

First, there's the relentless focus on examinations and standardised testing. As schoolkids, we stop asking questions born of genuine interest and instead ask, "Is this going to be in the test?" We focus on what will be measured and marked, not on what might expand our understanding.

Second, there's the disconnect between learning and application. "How will this help us in the real world?" was one of my favourite questions in maths class. It was a legitimate query about the relevance of derivatives, integers, and quadratic equations. I rarely got a satisfactory answer. Usually, I got told to be quiet. I was immensely curious, but that curiosity was socially unacceptable, so I learned to keep my questions to myself.

We're training our brains to skim, not to wonder and ponder.

It's not just school structure that impacts our questions, but our changing social habits too. A massive U.S. study of teenagers in 2016 found that one in three 18-year-olds hadn't read a single book for pleasure in the past year — nearly three times the rate of non-readers in the 1970s. It's not just a shift from paper to screens either, but a drop in reading *any* long–form content. We've replaced it with short-form scrolling, clicks, and swipes. We're training our brains to skim, not to wonder and ponder.

But does this decline in questions matter? And does our curiosity die as we grow older, or do we merely express it in different ways? The same person who sits silently in meetings might spend hours at night exploring new recipes, researching travel destinations, or learning about classic cars. Are they lacking curiosity or are they merely keeping themselves out of trouble at work? Just because my children ask more questions than me, does that mean they are more curious?

The research on this is surprisingly clear. "Curiosity rises into middle age before tapering gently later," explains curiosity researcher Todd Kashdan.

The difference between children and adults, he suggests, is *how* we display our curiosity. Children display it externally; their questions are confetti. We adults, on the other hand, tend to internalise our curiosity. But just because we don't ask as many questions, that doesn't mean we're not as curious. Often, there are a bunch of other factors that prevent us from externalising our curiosity — not the least of which is that many of us don't appreciate the value of going deeper with our questions in the first place.

Curiosity enables contribution

In 1956, an IKEA employee named Gillis Lundgren faced a practical problem. He needed to transport a bulky table to a photo shoot for the company's catalogue, but it wouldn't fit into his car. Depending on which source you read, he either patiently unscrewed or feverishly sawed away the table's legs. This makeshift solution would unexpectedly transform both IKEA and the entire furniture industry.

Ingvar Kamprad, who had founded IKEA thirteen years earlier, immediately saw the potential. If customers could transport and assemble furniture themselves, IKEA could dramatically reduce shipping costs and damage during transport.

People value things more when they've played a part in creating them.

The flat-pack revolution was born, though not without scepticism from competitors. Industry experts scoffed at the idea that customers would assemble their own furniture. Who would want to spend their weekend wrestling with screws and Allen wrenches when they could buy pre-assembled pieces?

Those sceptics were soon eating their words. Rather than

resenting the assembly process, many customers appeared to *enjoy* it. More surprisingly still, they seemed to develop a stronger attachment to the furniture they had built themselves. (Although there does always seem to be at least one screw left over — just to keep us guessing.)

Kamprad observed this phenomenon but couldn't fully explain it. It would be decades before researchers confirmed what IKEA had stumbled upon: people value things more when they've played a part in creating them. In a 2012 study, Harvard researchers Michael Norton, Daniel Mochon, and Dan Ariely dubbed this 'the IKEA effect'.

They figured this out in an experiment where participants either built a simple IKEA storage box or received a pre-assembled box. When asked how much they would pay for the box, those who built it themselves were willing to pay five times more than those who received a pre-assembled box. More tellingly, they expected others to value them just as highly too.

But what's the relevance for us as leaders? When people help to develop solutions, they value those solutions more highly. They feel greater ownership and commitment. They're more motivated to see things succeed.

This is the power of The Question Effect. When we ask rather than tell, we create mini 'IKEA effect' moments — opportunities for people to contribute to solutions they'll value more highly.

A social superpower

There's another compelling reason to embrace question-led leadership, which I wasn't expecting to find in the research.

It turns out that asking questions dramatically improves the quality of our relationships.

As you read the scenario below, I'd like you to consider: Who is making the better impression?

Let's say two colleagues strike up a conversation at a work function. Andrea tells a funny story about her previous job. Ben is interested and engaged, asking questions that encourage Andrea to elaborate. After the story ends, they exchange pleasantries and part ways.

Who do you think will have made the better impression? Andrea the storyteller or Ben the asker?

A group of psychologists studied this exact scenario through a series of controlled conversations. In some, they instructed one person to ask a lot of questions; in others, to ask few or no questions.

They published their results in a paper entitled quite plainly: "It doesn't hurt to ask: Question-asking increases liking." The effect was especially strong when they asked follow-up questions that showed they were truly listening. It's just like that cliched Hollywood scenario. A couple goes on a date and the man talks about himself non-stop, asking not a single question. We all know there will be no second date!

Curiosity thrives in the uncomfortable space between knowing and not knowing.

Now, you might be thinking, "That's great, but I'm leading, not dating." Yet how much of leadership depends on relationships and influence? The quality of our relationships dictates so many of our results – whether it's our relationships with staff, customers, clients, community members or social media followers. Showing up with curiosity is the key to building and maintaining these relationships, although this is getting harder to do in our busy lives.

The three curiosity categories

What makes curiosity such a powerful leadership tool is that it thrives precisely where most of us feel uncomfortable: in the space between knowing and not knowing. While our instinct is often to eliminate uncertainty as quickly as possible, curiosity invites us to linger there a little longer. It's the willingness to sit with questions before rushing to answers.

This uncertain territory is where we can make the biggest impact as leaders – whether in an awkward conversation, a challenging meeting or a project that's gone off the rails. When we try to rush past the discomfort of not knowing, we might miss opportunities that only emerge when we dig a little deeper. Curiosity is our guide through that ambiguous space.

Fittingly, there's no agreed scientific definition of curiosity. But I find it useful to divide it into three categories that serve different purposes in our lives:

Cognitive curiosity is the mind's quest for knowledge. It's what propels us to read books, take courses, and solve puzzles.

Sensory curiosity is the body's attraction to novelty. It drives us toward new stimuli and experiences, like a magpie drawn to a shiny object. It's why I encourage teams to have big conversations outside their office. A fresh environment awakens the senses, helping us to have a different conversation.

Finally, **empathic curiosity** is our heart's interest in others. Why else would TV shows like *Friends* or *Married at First Sight* be so popular? The entertainment stems from the relationships and drama along the way.

Experiential Activity 3B: Three Curiosity Categories

Let's experience the three curiosity categories:

- **Cognitive:** Close your eyes and reflect on your experience reading this book so far. How has reading impacted your mood or energy?
- **Sensory:** Tune into the sounds around you. What do you notice? How does noticing impact you?
- **Empathic:** Imagine what the person nearest to you is feeling right now. How does noticing this impact you?

These three types of curiosity are in full swing in my three-year-old son. He's obsessed with puzzles (cognitive curiosity); he loves getting his hands dirty in flour, mud, and leaves (sensory curiosity); and he's forever telling us about the shifting friendship dynamics at his kindergarten (empathic curiosity). These three types of curiosity provide different ways for him to explore and make sense of the world.

It doesn't matter what the problem is, curiosity is the answer.

Can we say the same for people sitting in offices tapping away at keyboards and whiling away their hours in meetings? When we don't allow people to explore their curiosity, we limit their capacity to find novel solutions to tough problems. It's like praying for rain instead of digging some wells.

It doesn't matter what the problem is, curiosity is the answer. This might sound simplistic, but I've found it to be profoundly true. Each type of curiosity fuels a different ripple of The Question Effect — whether it's sharper ideas (cognitive), fresher perspectives (sensory), or deeper connection (empathic). By activating a different kind of curiosity, we can guide people towards solutions that might otherwise remain undiscovered.

Curious Questions: Set 3B

Take a moment to explore how curiosity shows up in your work:

- Which curiosity category do you use most often — cognitive, sensory, or empathic?
- Which would you like to use more? How might you practise it?
- How culturally acceptable is it to be curious in your workplace?

Curiosity makes ideas stick

Ever wonder why some ideas stick — while others evaporate the moment people leave the room? Too often, in our attempts to keep things 'professional', we strip away the very thing that makes learning memorable. We avoid drama and polish our presentations and documents until everything feels smooth — yet painfully forgettable.

And the problem is that bored minds don't learn. Curiosity changes that. In fact, when we spark curiosity, we're rewiring people's brains to learn better.

That might sound like wishful thinking, but neuroscience backs it up. A research team at the University of California set out to test this in a wonderful experiment. They asked volunteers to rate how curious they were about the answers to trivia questions like "What does the term 'dinosaur' mean?" and "What Beatles' single lasted longest on the charts?"[1]

Using functional MRI scanning, they tracked what happened in people's brains. When people felt curious, two key regions lit up:

- The reward system: flooding the brain with dopamine, the same feel–good chemical we get when ticking tasks off a list.
- The hippocampus: the part of the brain responsible for forming new memories.

The researchers went even further. While people were answering the trivia questions, they secretly flashed up photos of random strangers unrelated to the questions. Later, when asked to recall those faces, participants remembered far more of them *if they'd been curious* about the trivia question when the face appeared.

In other words, curiosity about one thing made people remember something completely different. It's as if curiosity opens a wider gate in the brain, letting more information through — even stuff we're not consciously focused on.

> Curiosity about one thing made people remember something completely different.

---

[1] So you're reading this footnote? Huzzah! We've just proved the point. You couldn't help yourself. And now you're more likely to remember the power of curiosity too because this is a sneaky writing trick, isn't it? As for the answers, Sir Richard Owen coined the word dinosaur in 1841 by smooshing two Greek words together to mean "fearfully-great lizard", while 'Hey Jude' was the longest running Beatles' single.

Experiential Activity 3C: The Curiosity Gap

Lift up one arm to parallel and swivel so you're pointing as far behind your back as you can.

With your eyes, take note of a spot just a little further than where your finger is pointing. Turn back to the front.

Now do the activity again. Can you reach the point just beyond your original reach?

Most people can — and that's the power of curiosity. Questions create a gap and challenge our brains to go further.

This explains why some lessons stick with us for decades while others fade from memory within days. It's why we can recall intricate details from novels that captivated us years ago but struggle to remember a single detail from that dry first aid course we took last month. Curiosity is a cognitive super-glue. It helps ideas stick. As leaders, when we spark curiosity, we're priming people's brains to better absorb, process, and retain information.

Why don't we ask more?

Have you ever felt a question bubble up, but then you've stopped yourself from asking it? You're not alone. We often have the curiosity but we lack the conditions and permissions to express it. Through my work with leaders and teams, I've noticed five familiar patterns that prevent us from asking questions — even when we feel that spark of interest:

1. We overestimate how smart we are

I saw some amusing research that shines a light on this. Marshall Goldsmith, an American leadership coach and researcher, has surveyed over 50,000 leaders through his company Best Practice. In one section, they asked each leader to rate themselves relative to their professional peers. You can only laugh at the results:

- About 60% of all leaders rank themselves in the "top 10%" of their professional peer group
- Almost 85% say they are in the "top 20%"
- Over 98% claim to be in the "top half".

I'm no mathematician, but those numbers don't add up! We can't all be in the top 50%!

This happens because of the self-serving bias. This is the tendency to attribute good results to ourselves ("I worked hard" or "I'm smart") and poor results to others ("They were unreasonable" or "The project was impossible anyway").

We become delusional about how right we are, argues Goldsmith. And so — why would we ask?

2. We don't want to rock the boat

I once worked as a waiter for a restaurant owner whose approach could be summed up as 'my way or the highway.' My first day began with her screaming at me for being late (I was 5 minutes early). One day, she stabbed all the plastic milk bottles in anger, leaving a milky white flood for an employee to clean up.

In environments like this, questions become risks. I sweated for weeks over whether or not to ask the owner: "What's our reason for charging customers 50 cents for extra sauce?" That question felt like a major act of rebellion in that workplace. I didn't want to rock the boat, so I kept quiet, even though the policy infuriated our customers.

3. We're too busy

I once spoke at an engineering company's leadership forum and the retiring CEO said that every major regret in his career stemmed from his failure to ask hard questions. When I asked him what held his questions back, he said he was usually trying to avoid more work.

I totally understand this. You might think about asking a question, but then worry you'll get this response: "Good question, why don't you look into that?" Asking risks you getting lumped with even more work — exactly what we don't need when we're already busy.

4. We don't want to look stupid

One of the things I love about being a consultant is people accept that I'll need to ask lots of questions. The same is true for new employees. But eventually, that 'permission' starts to disappear in our minds. After six months in a role, we might feel embarrassed to ask about the acronym or question a daft policy decision we probably ought to know about by now. Better to keep our mouth closed and have people suspect we're ignorant than to open our mouths and confirm it, right?

5. We don't want to waste everybody's time

Have you ever heard somebody say: "Look, I don't want to take us off track, but..."? It's a protective phrase we use when we're worried about consuming time. We fear using valuable minutes in busy meetings. Sometimes this concern is legitimate, but other times it can become an excuse to avoid deeper exploration. After all, how much wasted effort might we avoid with a question that prevents a risk from becoming a reality?

Curiosity as an antidote

Each of those barriers blunts The Question Effect before it can ripple out, and this creates a vicious cycle of apathy:

- When we're stressed or scared, it's harder to be curious.
- Without curiosity, we struggle to find new solutions.
- Without novel solutions, problems get worse.
- Worse problems mean more stress and worry.

And on and on we go.

But research suggests curiosity itself can break this cycle. I found a fascinating study where researchers tracked 167 people over 21 days, asking them to journal each day. They found that when people felt curious, they were much less distressed by stressful events. It's like curiosity gave them a sort of emotional shield.

On the other side of the equation, curiosity creates a virtuous cycle:

- When we're curious, we spot possibilities we'd otherwise miss.
- These new possibilities often lead to better solutions.
- Better solutions mean fewer problems weighing us down.
- With that weight lifted, we can afford to remain curious.

And upward we go.

The good news is this virtuous cycle of The Question Effect has two self-reinforcing qualities.

The first happens through the psychological principle of priming. Now that we understand the importance of curiosity, we're more likely to notice opportunities for curiosity every day. It's like when we purchase a new car and suddenly see that model everywhere. We haven't magically influenced the car market — we're just primed to notice what was already there. In the same way, learning about the importance of curiosity primes our brains to spot moments where a question might be more valuable than an answer.

When we're curious, others around us become more curious too.

Secondly, curiosity spreads through emotional contagion. When we're curious, others around us become more curious too. One person asking thoughtful questions can transform a stale meeting into an energising exploration. One team modelling curiosity can shift an entire department's approach to problems.

This might help explain why some teams bounce back from setbacks while others crumble. Teams that maintain curiosity — that keep exploring and questioning even when things get tough — seem to develop a collective resilience. They don't get stuck in that vicious cycle of stress and narrowed thinking.

The impact goes beyond teams too. Curious people are more likely to engage with ideas they disagree with — not to argue, but to understand. The curious mind thinks: "That's not what I believe… but I wonder why they see it that way?"

As Jonathan Haidt, author of multiple books on morality, explains: the loss of curiosity is the big step towards a society breaking down because it leads us away from healthy disagreement and towards unhealthy disconnection.

If curiosity has a superpower, it's that it builds bridges in a world full of impassable rivers. The moments when we most want to cling to answers are precisely when questions become most valuable. When it feels like everything is falling apart, The Question Effect shines a light to help us find our way forward.

Curious Questions: Set 3C

Let's explore how curiosity could make a difference for you:

- Where in your life would you like to be more curious?
- What benefits could come from being more curious?
- What's one small step you could take to be more curious, more often?

Remember, you can download a printable workbook for these at paulmcgregor.co.nz/question-effect-toolkit

---

Questions worth asking

As we close Part 1, let's reflect on The Question Effect so far. By now, it's clear that our questions go into hiding as we grow older — not because we lose curiosity, but because questioning becomes less socially expected. And yet the evidence shows that questions build stronger relationships, reduce our leadership burden, and enable better outcomes.

Curiosity comes in different flavours — cognitive, sensory, and empathic — and knowing this can help us address the barriers that keep curiosity hidden underground. Perhaps most importantly, questions can break the vicious cycle of apathy and create a virtuous cycle of engagement instead.

In Part 2, we'll move from the *why* to the *what* — exploring specific questions that create better outcomes through bigger conversations. That's not to say that these are the *only* questions we should ask or that they're magical spells that will dissolve every leadership challenge. But they're a great place to start.

Are you curious about the sorts of questions that can drive meaningful change? Let's find out together.

Part 2

LEADING QUESTIONS

CHAPTER 4

Seven leadership
challenges

Seven leading questions

"My greatest strength as a consultant is to be ignorant and ask a few questions."

– Peter Drucker

magine you walk into a doctor's office with chest pains. Instead of examining you or asking about your symptoms, she immediately says: "I see you've done some research online. You think you need a heart stent? Let's schedule that surgery right away."

You'd be alarmed — and rightfully so. A good doctor would first ask questions to understand your symptoms. She'd inquire about your medical history, lifestyle, and when the pain started. She might schedule a collection of tests or refer you to several specialists. Only after this careful assessment would the surgery be booked — if at all.

Yet this is precisely what we do when we jump to conclusions and solve the first problem that presents itself in the workplace. We skip the discovery phase entirely, rushing to solutions before we understand what's really happening.

I learned this lesson the hard way as a young consultant. I was ecstatic when I won my first client project. Our task was to enable a government agency to identify new ways of helping young people to get physically active. We hosted an initial workshop and a few days later emailed an insights report to the agency leaders — inviting them to discuss the next phase. We waited. And waited. I emailed. I called.

Eventually, the uncomfortable truth dawned on me: they weren't interested in following through. We had mined young people for their ideas and taken some photos for good PR — and now the agency had moved on to other priorities. The real but messy work of building relationships and creating stuff together never eventuated. Those young people were left behind while the executives ticked 'youth engagement' off their list.

I was so embarrassed. The community leaders had warned me this would happen, and their concerns had come true. "Paul's a really good guy," one of them wrote in an email, "But I just don't think this project was that well thought through."

What went wrong? Quite simply, I was so eager to secure the work that I danced lightly through the discovery phase. I wrongly assumed we all wanted the same thing. I didn't ask enough questions to dig under the surface to reveal people's true intentions and the deeper issues.

The solution isn't more questions; it's better ones.

Yet there's also a tension here. Nobody wants to be *that person* who asks so many questions they derail everything. We've all been around people who keep taking things off track, leaving everyone checking their watches and wishing for their lunch break.

The solution isn't more questions; it's better ones. Certain questions have the power to shift conversations and lead groups toward meaningful change. I call these Leading Questions.

Questions that lead

You probably already know the difference between closed and open questions:

- Closed questions invite yes or no answers ("Did you enjoy the meeting?").
- Open questions invite elaboration ("What did you think of the meeting?").

Both have their place. I most commonly use closed questions at the start and end of conversations. They're typically quite easy to answer and this can open people up when you first start talking. They also help to clarify details towards the end of a conversation. Open questions are perfect in the middle of a conversation when people are warmed up and the conversation is flowing nicely.

But what, then, are Leading Questions? A Leading Question does two important things simultaneously:

- It contains a powerful idea, and
- It encourages meaningful conversation around that idea.

Leading Questions aren't manipulative tricks to get people to do what you want, like the witness interrogation techniques I learned in law school. Rather, they're invitations to explore important territory together. They function like well-designed trails through complex terrain — offering direction while allowing for discovery.

I began to realise their power through mentoring other leaders. At the end of mentoring sessions, I would often ask: "What was the most valuable part of today's session for you?" And people kept talking about specific questions I had shared with them.

Seven critical leadership challenges

In the following chapters, we're going to explore seven leadership challenges where the right question can have an outsized impact. Our instinct often pulls us toward giving answers, when asking might serve us better in these sorts of situations.

Here's a glimpse of the Leading Questions we'll explore:

	The Question	The Idea
Vision	What would a good ancestor do?	Visionaries look generations ahead, not years ahead.
Strategy	What can we say 'no' to so we can say 'yes' to what matters?	What you don't do determines what you can do well.
Culture	What will help us be the people we want to be?	People who feel valued add more value.
Perspectives	Whose voices are missing?	Diverse perspectives ensure better outcomes.
Experience	What little things will make them feel big?	Small details have an outsized impact.
Conflict	What's really going on here?	Conflict is always about something deeper.
Learning	What's a small and safe way to test that?	Small risks address big risks.

These questions aren't magic formulas to be recited robotically. They're starting points that invite us into deeper conversations. They work because they contain both wisdom (a perspective) and humility (a question). Ultimately, they help us to have bigger conversations – leading us to better outcomes.

In the chapters ahead, we'll explore each question in depth — the thinking behind it, why it works, when to use it, and how to adapt it to your context. Each question will help you think differently about these common leadership challenges — while also giving you a way to bring others into the conversation.

Curious Questions: Set 4

Let's make these seven challenges even more relevant for you:

- Which of these seven challenges do you feel most confident about? What makes you say that?
- Which one needs the most attention in your current work — and why?
- If you could get better at just one of these in the next six months, which would you choose — and what difference would it make?

Leading with questions doesn't mean abandoning your expertise or never sharing your perspective. It means starting conversations differently — with curiosity rather than certainty — and trusting that better solutions will emerge as a result.

To begin with, we'll start with one of the most fundamental leadership challenges: shaping a vision that transcends the immediate pressures of today. Let's start with The Vision Question.

CHAPTER 5

The Vision Question

*What would a good
ancestor do?*

"Where there is no vision, there is no hope."

– George Washington Carver

t was 2019, and community leaders had gathered to discuss the future of Te Tau Ihu — the top of the South Island of New Zealand where I live. The conversation had quickly descended into debates about pressing issues like which roads should be built next, how to manage water supplies, and what to do about housing affordability. Practical matters, certainly. Important ones, even. But something was missing.

The room hummed with the tension of competing priorities, each person advocating for their corner of concern. That's when one of the facilitators posed a different question:

"What would it mean to be a good ancestor?"

The room fell silent.

"We have a 500-year intergenerational vision," I later heard Miriana Stevens, one of the directors of Wakatū Incorporation, explain in a video on Te Kai a te Rangatira, a website dedicated to sharing Māori leadership perspectives. Wakatū has approximately 4,000 owners who all descend from Māori ancestors. They've grown from an $11 million asset base in 1977 to over $350 million today.

Miriana went on to explain that their 500-year vision is something they live and breathe every day. "It excites us. It scares us. But it's a way of being. When we look back 500 years from where we evolved and then 500 years into the future, it gives us a level of comfort and security that we do have a good future, as long as it's guided by our values."

Five hundred years? Who can possibly plan that far ahead?

I imagine the suggestion to think in 500-year terms, rather than 5-year terms, was a shock to many of the non-Māori in the room. Five hundred years? Who can possibly plan that far ahead? For local government, a Long-Term Plan is one that looks ten years out!

But that meeting marked the beginning of a shared inter-generational vision that continues to guide our region today. At its heart is the Māori concept of Tupuna Pono — being a good ancestor.

And it got me thinking: what if this kind of question — and this shift in timeframe — is exactly what we're missing in our frantic day-to-day leadership?

It's easy to get swept up in the rat race — hustling around with our heads down, just doing the work. As Peter Senge wrote in *The Fifth Discipline*, we live in a time where "cost and performance pressures are relentless" and "the time available for people to think and reflect is scarcer."

But what if the answer isn't more speed and efficiency? What if it's about asking a bigger question to see beyond today's urgent demands?

In this chapter, we'll explore why most leaders get vision wrong, some of the ways indigenous cultures approach long-term thinking, and, most importantly, how we can use vision questions to transform our organisations today, not just tomorrow.

This kind of generational thinking might initially seem impractical, but as we'll discover, it's exactly what our short-term focused world desperately needs.

What is vision?

Have you ever found yourself in an argument about the difference between vision, mission, purpose, strategy, and culture? No? Just me?

As a consultant, I used to facilitate lots of big picture conversations for organisations large and small — in business, government, and community settings. Early on, I noticed that we kept getting side-tracked with arguments about the definitions — usually about half-way through the process when we *ought* to have been making some tough decisions.

I saw this play out vividly with Hato Hone St John, New Zealand's largest charity. Their Community Health and Engagement Directorate had been operating with a 70+ page vision and strategy document filled with detailed targets and goals. The head of the directorate, Sarah Manley, approached us with a clear goal: create a four-page document that captured the essence of their vision.

As we began the work, we quickly discovered part of the problem. The massive document mixed concepts freely and nobody quite knew what to refer to or when. It made it nearly impossible for people to prioritise or make decisions quickly — the exact reason why the document existed.

This challenge wasn't unique to St John. I've seen countless other leadership teams struggle with the same confusion. So, I decided we needed to come to the table with some stronger definitions of these key terms. Today, I use the analogy of an ocean–going journey to illustrate the differences:

- Vision is *where* we want to go. It's the horizon that pulls us forward, even in stormy weather.

- Purpose is *why* we want to go. It's the driving force in our gut that tells us to risk it all.
- Strategy is *how* we'll get there. It's the boat we choose to sail.
- Mission is *what* we'll do to get there. It's the daily routine of trimming the sails and keeping the boat ship–shape.
- Culture is *the way* we'll do it. The songs we sing while we're working; the jokes we tell; the stories shared at night; the meetings on deck — all the things that other boats might think are unusual, but which need no explanation on our boat.

I don't think it matters which definitions we use, but that we agree on some together and use them consistently. All the same, I wish we had this sort of clarity when starting the St John project. It might have saved us a lot of angst, although those challenging discussions did lead us towards a valuable outcome. As Sarah later told me: "The process has lit a fire under our team, and I can see it coming through every day." It wasn't just a shorter document, but a more meaningful one.

This experience reinforced what I'd learned from that Te Tau Ihu meeting. Vision isn't about perfect wording or lengthy documents. It's about capturing the essence of where we're heading in a way that moves people to action.

Generations, not quarters

The question about being a good ancestor was powerful because it fundamentally shifted the timeframe and with it, the decisions that followed. It may have surprised many of the non-Māori in the room that day, but anybody familiar with the Māori worldview would have understood the deeper philosophy.

In the book *Belonging: The Ancient Code of Togetherness*, Owen Eastwood explains the Māori concept of whakapapa:

> *"Each of us is part of an unbreakable chain of people, back into our past to our first ancestors, and into the future, to the end of time. Everybody has their arms interlocked so it's an unbreakable chain. The metaphor is that the sun first shone on our origin story and slowly moves down this chain of people, and when the sun shines on you that signifies your time."*

When we think of the world this way, five or ten years no longer seems long-term. It's merely a blip in the scheme of generations.

Māori are not the only culture to embrace such a long-term view of vision. The Seventh Generation Principle is a concept of the Six Nations confederacy in North America (also known as the Haudenosaunee or the Iroquois people). The principle states that leaders should consider how their actions will affect the welfare of the seventh generation into the future. If we assume that a generation is about 20 years, this means looking 140 years ahead.

Now, I know what you're thinking: "That's all well and good for indigenous cultures with centuries of tradition, but I have quarterly targets to hit!"

You're right — and that's exactly the problem. The timeframe we choose fundamentally changes the decisions we make. So, before we dismiss long–term visioning as idealistic or impractical, let's take a closer look at what changes when we stretch our timeframe.

Experiential Activity 5: The Three Horizons

After you've read these instructions, I invite you to close your eyes:

- Picture your work one year from now. What comes into focus?
- Now picture it 15 years from now. What do you notice?
- Finally, imagine it 150 years from now. What comes to mind?

How did the timeframe influence what you imagined?

Vision questions are time machines

One of the most common ways that scientists test human decision-making tendencies is through something called the 'k-arm bandit task'. The name comes from the 'one-armed bandit' — an old name for slot machines.

In these experiments, you face multiple options with different payoffs, similar to a gambler facing several slot machines with hidden payout rates. The 'k' simply refers to the number of options available. A '2-arm bandit' gives us two choices, while a '10-arm bandit' gives us ten.

Researchers love these tests because they capture a fundamental dilemma we face every day: should we stick with something good or risk it all for something better?

Imagine taking this test yourself. You're presented with a series of random images to choose from. At the start, you have no way of knowing which images will score high and which will score low. To get a good score, you need to balance two strategies: exploration and exploitation. When exploring, you select a new image to discover its value. When exploiting, you choose an image you already know scores well.

One of the most powerful findings from these studies is this:

"With longer horizons, subjects were more likely to choose an exploratory strategy than an exploitative one."

What does this mean for leadership exactly? When people are rushed, we make poor decisions. We act out of fear rather than optimism. In short, we waste time, money, and energy on things that might have little benefit in the long

The timeframe we choose fundamentally changes the decisions we make.

run. But when we feel we have more time, we're more willing to sacrifice short-term rewards for greater long-term results.

That's the power of a vision question. By extending our timeframe — whether it's from one year to five, or from decades to generations — we fundamentally shift how we approach decisions today.

Visionary thinking for busy people

Did you know that most office workers spend more time getting themselves ready to work than actually working? That's according to Asana's Anatomy of Work Index, which surveyed around 10,000 knowledge workers from around the globe and found we spend about 60% of our days on coordination: checking email, updating systems, looking for information, arranging meetings, trying not to fall asleep in those meetings...

All this coordination leaves us feeling like we barely have

time for our actual work, let alone anything visionary. So, when somebody asks us to step into a big-picture conversation about the future, it feels indulgent — like a luxury we cannot afford. We haven't got time to do our day job, let alone imagine the future. The gap between here and there feels too big to even contemplate.

But the tension is that the busier we get, the *more* we need visionary thinking, not less. Visionary thinking isn't something to do once a year at a retreat. It should inform our daily decisions. Without it, we risk becoming extremely efficient at doing the wrong things. However, the pressure for immediate results is real, and advocating for long-term thinking can feel like swimming against a powerful current.

If you're stuck in a reactive environment with short planning cycles, here are some things that might help.

First, try extending the timeframes just a little bit. Don't try to leap from quarterly thinking to multi-generational thinking. If your organisation currently operates on a one-year horizon, first stretch to three years, then five. These small extensions create far less resistance than proposing radical shifts all at once.

Make the future tangible through stories. Abstract futures don't pull on the heartstrings enough. To address this, try developing two or three detailed future scenarios that bring potential outcomes to life. When people can imagine different futures, they become much more invested in shaping them.

Start small to build credibility. If you're meeting strong resistance, start with just a single project rather than trying to shift your entire organisation's timeframe. Create a 'future-focused initiative' with its own longer timeframe. Success in this contained environment builds credibility for extending timeframes more broadly.

Resistance to long-term thinking is often more emotional than intellectual. Most people intuitively understand the value of thinking ahead. The challenge is creating an environment where doing so feels safe, valuable, and rewarded.

Curious Questions: Set 5

These questions will help you use vision questions more effectively in your work:

- What vision (formal or informal) guides your work right now?
- How do people typically respond when you discuss that vision?
- How could you express that vision in a leading question?
- When and where could you ask a vision question like that?

Vision Questions turn us into futurists

The immediate challenges we face today are often the result of short-term thinking from yesterday. Climate collapse, polarised societies, and crumbling infrastructure weren't caused by people thinking too far ahead but by generations of leaders focused on the next quarter, election, or news cycle.

Many of these challenges are symptoms of a society experiencing growth pains. We're in the early years of the so-called Fourth Industrial Revolution and we're seeing the early impacts. The previous three revolutions — steam in the early 1700s, electricity in the late 1800s, and digital in the 1900s — brought tectonic shifts in how we live, work, and play.

The Fourth Industrial Revolution is already blurring the lines between the physical, digital, and biological realms. Recent advancements in AI, machine learning, robotics, the Internet of Things, 3D printing, and big data are just the beginning.

But what is this fourth industrial revolution? Is it the AI revolution? The automation revolution? Right now, even though we're in the middle of the revolution, it's still challenging to know its true nature. Anybody who claims to know where all this change is taking us is either ignorant, lying to you, selling you something – or all three!

All we can do in the face of such change is stay grounded in what we value — in what is important to us. That's what vision questions help us to do. They turn us into futurists by shifting our focus from today to tomorrow — to the legacy we leave our descendants. In a world of dramatically conflicting forces, is there any shift more important than that?

As we look ahead to the next chapter on strategy, remember that vision sets our destination, but strategy determines our path. Without a clear vision of where we're headed, even the best strategy might lead us somewhere we never intended to go. The Vision Question — What would a good ancestor do? — creates the foundation upon which all our other decisions can rest.

CHAPTER 6

The Strategy Question

What can we say 'no' to so we can say 'yes' to what matters?

"So often people are working hard at the wrong thing."

– Caterina Fake

Every year, organisations invest millions into strategic plans. They are meant to be a salve to the busyness we all face at work – a way to step back, gain clarity, and make better choices about where to focus our limited time and energy. But how valuable are they? Far too often, they're often frustrating at best, and pointless at worst.

Here's how it typically unfolds.

A flurry of workshops is arranged. A survey goes out to all staff, along with customers, partners, vendors, and funders. Your insights team reviews all the most recent data and research, meticulously preparing a 70–page report outlining recent trends.

Before long, you're drowning in information, with hundreds of suggestions, concerns, and opportunities to wade through.

You sort everything into categories, each with five to fifteen ideas beneath them — and that's just the first half of the document. You present everything to your board, who carefully shift ideas between categories, adding metrics, and spending hours debating whether to use the term 'strategic priorities' or 'pillars of impact'.

Everybody breathes a sigh of relief when it's over — and promptly goes back to doing their jobs once again.

Then somebody complains it's too complex. A one-pager gets prepared. When you print it out, you can barely read the size-nine font.

Everybody breathes a sigh of relief when it's over — and promptly goes back to doing their jobs once again.

That ain't strategy, it's wishful thinking.

For all that work, you haven't made any real trade-offs or touched any of the sacred cows. You've tidily organised everything you're currently doing and added a bunch of new things you'd like to do (pending no minor disasters).

A version of this scenario plays out in organisations everywhere because most of us have never been taught what strategy is. And when we're constantly busy, we lack the headspace to think things through effectively. When the moment comes, we're too drained and worried to make the hard choices that real strategy demands.

The Strategy Question — What can we say 'no' to so we can say 'yes' to what matters? — cuts through this confusion by forcing us to confront the fundamental challenge of strategy: making tough choices.

I've worked with dozens of leadership teams on strategy, and I've experienced three common strategy mistakes that consistently trip us all up. Let's start with the most fundamental problem: most of us don't know what strategy is.

Mistake 1: Mistaking planning for strategy

The root of the word *strategy* comes from Greek, where it basically means army leader or general. Over time, the word evolved and became part of corporate language, where it referred to the art and science of directing large-scale operations.

We love the word. Whenever we want to make anything

sound important or smart, we'll pop *strategic* next to it. *Strategic* investments. *Strategic* Relationship Manager. *Strategic* offsite. I wonder if we shouldn't just replace it with the word *important*.

A good strategy has a kernel

But how do we know if we're being strategic or not? I've always valued this guidance from Richard Rumelt in his book *Good Strategy, Bad Strategy*:

> *"A good strategy has an essential logical structure that I call the kernel... It is like a signpost, marking the direction forward but not defining the details of the trip."*

If a good strategy has a kernel — a core idea that points us in the right direction — then we should be able to sum it up in a sentence or three. I'm sorry but if we need to open a long document to explain our strategy, then we don't have a strategy; there's obviously no kernel.

If we need to open a long document to explain our strategy, then we don't have a strategy.

The real test of strategy is whether it helps you when faced with choices. A good strategy gives us a clear filter for what to pursue and what to pass up. To put it in my own words, a good strategy needs to be:

- **Decisive:** It makes bold choices about what matters and what doesn't.
- **Memorable:** We can remember it without effort.
- **Useful:** People actually use it to influence their daily work.

Rediscovering Lego's roots

One of my favourite strategies comes from the toy-maker Lego, which I discovered in Alex MH Smith's *Strategy Secrets* series. I loved Lego as a kid, although I love it less now when I'm continually tripping over pieces left around our house every night.

In the 1990s, Lego was struggling. They had become just–another–toy–brand. On the shelves, there was little to distinguish them from all the other toy boxes at Christmas time. In fact, they were less exciting than many of the new video game offerings.

In 1994, their new CEO Vig Knudstorp realised that Lego had forgotten its roots: teaching kids how to create things. The brand had originally established itself as an educational tool, not an entertaining toy, and they had lost sight of this.

In essence, Knudstorp asked The Strategy Question: What should Lego say 'no' to so they could say 'yes' to what mattered most? The answer was to say 'yes' to educational experiences. This led to Lego partnering with educators, promoting Lego for fine motor skills in nurseries, linking with engineering and robotics in secondary schools, and even building a Lego science, technology, engineering and maths (STEM) qualification for kids.

Today, Lego is the most valuable toy brand in the world —
valued at $7.4 billion in 2023, with its closest toymaker rival
miles back at only $1.6 billion.

Can you see the power of having a clear kernel — a unifying
idea that influences people's decisions every day? Lego's strategy ticks all three boxes:

- **Is it decisive?** Yes, it says that educational value is the
  most important thing. This makes it easy to say 'no' to
  ideas that don't support learning.
- **Is it memorable?** Yes, everybody can remember
  the core idea of educational value. We don't need to
  read a long document or refer to a flow chart to get
  the concept.
- **Is it useful?** Yes, almost everybody in the organisation can use educational value as a filter for
  multiple decisions. It's not limited to just one part of
  the organisation.

Of course, having a clear kernel at the heart of your strategy
sounds great. But how do you achieve that when you're already
working too hard and barely have time to eat lunch every day?

Mistake 2: In the weeds

Back in 2020, I interviewed strategy expert Alicia McKay for
the *Beyond Consultation Podcast*.

"Why do we find strategy so hard?" I asked her.

"Oh, that's easy," she responded. "We're all so busy. We're
all trying to jam 60 to 80 hours' worth of work into a 40-hour
container every week. Creating the space to just go, 'What's all
this?' is really hard to do and it's not valued."

She went on to say, "Meaningfully creating intentional strategic space is the key responsibility of a senior leader and it's also the thing that we are least good at prioritising in the calendar."

> It's so easy to get trapped in what I call "false urgency" — constantly responding to whatever demands our immediate attention.

Her words resonated deeply, as I've seen this pattern everywhere. It's so easy to get trapped in what I call "false urgency" — constantly responding to whatever demands our immediate attention, rather than working on what would make the biggest difference long-term.

The Leadership Leverage Ladder

To understand why this happens, I've found it helpful to think about leadership as existing on a hierarchy — from low–leverage activities that *feel* urgent up to high–leverage activities that change how we see the world.

Role	Leverage	Stance	Focus
Leader	High	Creating Space	Possibilities
			Priorities
Manager	Medium	Holding Space	People
			Projects
Expert	Low	Taking Space	Problems
			Projects

Like any simplification, this model isn't the truth, but truth can emerge from the model. As you read through it, consider how you typically spend your time.

Let's break down each level in reverse order:

Practicalities are the administrative tasks that keep the wheels turning. This could be updating spreadsheets, booking transport, or filling in a form. They're the work equivalent of doing dishes: essential but not transformative.

Problems represent the firefighting many of us know far too well. Perhaps someone's upset about a decision, a project has hit a snag, or a customer is complaining. These feel urgent and important in the moment, but we're reacting to issues that have already materialised.

Projects give us a structure for coordinating resources and working towards a goal. Project work is valuable because it moves us forward. At the same time, it's tactical — focused on how to implement rather than what to implement.

People work is about getting the right talent on your team and making sure they can do good work. When you hire well and create a great environment, people solve problems before they flare up.

Priorities involve the strategic choices about what matters most. This is where we decide what to say 'yes' to and what to say 'no' to. This work has high leverage because our decisions influence the people, projects, problems, and practicalities that follow. This is where The Strategy Question sits.

Possibilities represent the highest leverage work — exploring future opportunities and imagining new ways of creating value. It often requires the most space and creative thinking, but it's worth it. This is the work of The Vision Question.

Experiential Activity 6B: The Leadership Leverage Ladder

Before we move on, I invite you to think about where you are investing your time as a leader. Use the ladder below to assess the difference between your current and ideal time split.

Level	Current %	Ideal %
Possibilities	_____ %	_____ %
Priorities	_____ %	_____ %
People	_____ %	_____ %
Projects	_____ %	_____ %
Problems	_____ %	_____ %
Practicalities	_____ %	_____ %

- How realistic is your ideal percentage split?
- What's one small shift you could make this month to move your time closer to your ideal?

False Urgency

The problem is our world is continually dragging our attention down the Ladder. When I introduce this model in workshops, most leaders say they spend anywhere from 50 to 80 percent of their time on Problems and Practicalities, the lowest-leverage activities.

It's totally understandable too. Our workplaces are loaded with distractions: emails, notifications, 'quick questions', lost documents... I could go on.

When I looked at the research on this, I found that we can basically divide our workdays into three parts:

- One third of our day is talking about work (emails and meetings).
- Another third is preparing for work (breaks, interruptions, searching for information).
- This leaves only one third for focused work.

It's critical that we protect that focused time. It's in that third that the opportunity sits for shifting up the Leadership Ladder.

This brings us back to Alicia's point about creating 'intentional strategic space'. We can't always expect somebody else to create that space for us; it's our responsibility to set the boundaries that allow us to pause, reflect, think, and reset – ideally every week, if not every day. This is where The Strategy Question becomes so powerful. By regularly asking "What can we say 'no' to so we can say 'yes' to what

> This fear of making trade–offs often leaves us without any clear direction at all.

matters?" we force ourselves to move up the hierarchy. Instead of reacting to what's in our faces, we're able to see new possibilities and choose the priorities that'll take us there.

Mistake 3: Avoiding hard choices

Even when we understand what strategy is and create space to think strategically, there's still one final trap: the temptation to include everything rather than choose what matters most.

This fear of making trade-offs often leaves us without any clear direction at all. We collect and categorise rather than choose.

As Alicia McKay said to me, "Good strategy requires us to turn things off, shut things down, piss people off, and just generally make hard trade-offs." This is precisely what The Strategy Question pushes us to do.

Of course, many of us don't like to make those tough choices. In an experiment conducted by the University of Waterloo, the researchers asked people to do something that went against their morals, such as damaging a library book. Even though they didn't agree with the task, about half of them ended up doing it anyway. That's because we despise saying "no" — even when we know we should. But why?

Mainly it's because we're wired to get along with others. Deep down, our brains still think that if people reject us, we might not survive. So, when we're about to say something that might upset someone, our body reacts. Our hands get sweaty, our hearts beat faster and we get that tight feeling in our throats. It's completely automatic; we can't *think* our way out of it.

Modern workplaces amplify this effect. We often reward agreement and cooperation more than healthy disagreement. We're praised for being 'team players' and taking on extra work, not for setting boundaries or questioning priorities.

The result is we say "yes" to everything, spreading our resources too thin and diluting our impact. True strategy becomes impossible because we're not incentivised to make hard choices about what deserves our focus and what doesn't.

Curious Questions: Set 6

Let's reflect on your capacity to make hard trade-offs as it's easier said than done:

- What's your personal relationship with the word 'no'?
- How acceptable is it to refuse work, shut down projects, or leave tasks unfinished in your workplace?
- What could make it easier for you to say 'no' when you need to?

The Power of a Positive No

A few years back, I was working in a highly toxic work environment where everybody was treading on eggshells around two key employees. I spent a lot of time at my local library looking for a way through. One of the most helpful books was William Ury's *The Power of a Positive No: How to Say No and Still Get to Yes*.

The basic premise of the book was simple. It was about saying 'no' without burning bridges through a tool that goes like this: "Yes! No. Yes?" Let me elaborate.

Yes!

First, we need to explain what we want to protect. What would you be losing if you said "yes"? Whatever is at the heart of your strategy — that's what we need to say "Yes!" to.

No.

Then we say 'no' or 'I can't', clearly and without insult.

Yes?

Finally, we offer an alternative way of addressing the issue.

I had the chance to put this into practice not long ago. A council official rang me asking me to lead a youth engagement event. It had been several years since I had done that sort of work and it was no longer a priority for me.

Here's how I should have answered him:

Yes!: "I'm focused on my speaking and coaching work at the moment."

No: "I'm not available for that sort of work."

Yes?: "Would you like me to refer you to a couple of other providers?"

That's what I *should* have said. In reality, I said "yes" on the call, kicked myself, and texted him 30 minutes later to politely decline. Knowing the theory is one thing: putting it into practice is another.

But the key message here is that saying "no" can be done nicely, in a way that doesn't burn bridges or leave you feeling like the bad guy. And it's a critical part of putting The Strategy Question to work. Without the ability to say "no", we easily fall prey to all the new opportunities and challenges that crop up every day, rather than staying focused on what we've already determined matters most.

Experiential Activity 6C: The Daily Directional

Strategy is something to live and breathe every day, not something to set and forget. If you're unsure how to do that, then you might benefit from The Daily Directional. It's a short 5-minute self-guided activity which I use every morning to set my focus and intention for the day.

It invites you to consider:

· Your energy from zero to ten
· Three things you're grateful for
· Your one big *yes* for the day
· Three *no's* to avoid that day
· Your intention for the day, expressed in a word.

It's a simple activity, but a powerful one. It brings the heady ideas of strategy into your ordinary workday – helping us to stay focused even when things keep changing.

You can access The Daily Directional and all other Question Effect resources at: **paulmcgregor.co.nz/question-effect-toolkit**.

Become discerning

The Strategy Question makes us discerning – a person who carefully selects what to do and what to leave. As Peter Drucker, a leading management theorist once said, "strategy is about omission."

When we're clear on our answer to The Strategy Question, it's a relief. Everything gets easier. We can focus our time and energy on what matters rather than trying to do everything.

But then your workplace culture may need to play catch up. If strategy is about making tough choices, then culture needs to support people when they make those choices. In the next chapter, we'll look at how to create a workplace where people can do their best work — a culture that helps our strategy succeed rather than fighting against it.

CHAPTER 7

The Culture Question

What will help us be the people we want to be?

"Culture can see further than strategy can imagine."

– Meredith Wilson

Have you ever worked in a toxic workplace culture? It's soul-destroying. It can turn the best of us into shells of our real selves.

I know this from experience. In the last decade, I've worked in more organisations than most people do in a lifetime: from large corporate behemoths to plucky little start-ups. In all those roles, culture was the primary reason I stayed – or departed early. Far too often, I found that the values on the wall bore little resemblance to people's behaviour. (The first time this struck me was in a law firm where I sat working in isolation — right next to the word "Collaboration" pasted in bold on the wall. Oh, the delicious irony.)

And I'm not alone. As a leadership coach, I've heard so many stories of people losing sleep, getting sick, and burning out in workplaces that make it incredibly challenging for good people to achieve the very thing they're employed to do.

Workplace culture is ten times more powerful than compensation when it comes to predicting why people quit.

Tony Schwartz, author of *The Way We're Working Isn't Working*, argues that we all have fundamental needs beyond just mental stimulation — we need to move our bodies, connect emotionally, and find meaning in our work. But most workplaces focus almost exclusively on cognitive performance. It's like our bodies are inconvenient transportation for our brains. Emotions? Check those at the door, please. And spiritual needs? Save that for your weekend.

Culture might sound like a soft issue, but the costs are

anything but. Disengagement carries a price tag of about $8.8 trillion globally, according to Gallup's research, due to low productivity, sick days, and unplanned turnover. Research from the MIT Sloan School of Management found that a toxic workplace culture is ten times more powerful than compensation when it comes to predicting why people quit. Ten times! In their review of 1.4 million employee reviews online, they found that people left mainly because they felt disrespected, excluded, or forced to work in ways that clashed with their values.

As leaders, this is great news. We can't increase people's pay every day, but we *can* influence culture every day. And that's what The Culture Question is all about: working on the conditions that shape behaviour, and improving them bit-by-bit, day-by-day.

But before we get to that, let's unpack what culture really means.

What culture really is

Culture is one of those words that gets thrown around so much it's almost lost its meaning. When I ask my coaching clients to describe it, they'll say things like:

- It's what people do when I'm not in the room
- It's how we behave
- It's our core values.

None of those answers are wrong per se, but they're only part of the picture. I like to think of culture as a mountain. The peak is aspirational: it's who we aspire to be. The foothills and valleys are practical: the places where we live and work every day. We need both the aspiration of the peak to orient us, and the discipline of everyday actions to keep moving us forward.

The Culture Question invites us to consider both:

- "What will help us..." - this points to our practical culture.
- "...be who we want to be?" - this points us to our aspirational culture.

Let's explore both aspects, one by one.

Culture as an aspiration

Many culture change efforts miss the mark because they focus only on aspirational values.

My experience at the Ministry of Justice summed this up perfectly. When I arrived, the values were printed on 1990s-style mouse pads: Respect. Integrity. Service. Excellence. A year later, the leadership team launched a 'values refresh' with advisory groups and feedback forums. The result was the same four values, but with prettier posters. Unsurprisingly, not much changed afterwards.

Part of the problem is that values are often so vague that they mean nothing. Consider a value like respect. Respect for what? For whom? When?

Value trade-offs

Let's return to my mountain metaphor. It's easy to point at the peak and say, "That's where we're heading." But climbing requires trade-offs. Which path should we take? Do we prioritise speed or views? Enjoyment or challenge?

This is why I always encourage my clients to go a step further than merely identifying a wish-list of preferred values. We also need to identify our value trade-offs. This means agreeing on what we value and what may come at that value's expense.

The easiest way to wrap your head around this is with the following sentence template:

We value [core value] over [another value] and even if [threat to the core value].

For instance, here's how that might have looked with the Ministry of Justice's values:

- We value respect over candour, and even if it means the truth takes longer to say.
- We value integrity over loyalty, and even if it means challenging those with power over us.
- We value service over efficiency, and even if it means saying 'no' to some requests.
- We value excellence over speed, and even if it means missing some opportunities.

Can you see how these statements force us to confront the trade-offs within our core values? They're uncomfortable to read out loud, but that's the point. They're honest. They're also far more valuable as a guide in stressful or overwhelming situations – the exact moments where we need our values the most.

Curious Questions: Set 7A

Before we move on, let's check the pulse of your organisational values:

- To what extent does everyday behaviour align with your stated values?
- When do people refer to your organisation's values (if at all)?
- How could you make your value trade-offs clearer?

Culture as practical actions

The aspirational side of culture may inspire us but it doesn't tell us what we should do. We've all experienced workplaces where the values on the wall have almost no correlation with the behaviour in the room. This is why the practical side of culture is so important.

I like how one of my mentors, Meredith Wilson, breaks it down in her book *Shift: Everyday Actions Leaders Can Take to Shift Culture*. She makes culture tangible through her GRASS framework:

G – gatherings. How do we bring people together? Those Monday morning meetings, the quarterly reviews, the Zoom calls that could've been emails...

R – rituals. How do we mark milestones? The way we welcome new people, celebrate wins, acknowledge failures, or say goodbye...

A – actions. What are the everyday habits we do without thinking? Late-night emails, eating at desks, helping colleagues without recognition, cleaning up common spaces...

S – symbols. What messages are hiding in plain sight? Our logos, the wall art, that old policy document on the wall from four years ago...

S – stories. What tales get told again and again? The legendary customer service win from five years ago, the time the founder stayed up all night to fix a client emergency, the cautionary tale of the last person to challenge the boss...

I would add two other elements to Meredith's mix:

E – environment. Where are we working? The tables, meeting rooms, desk types, lighting... Our environment shapes our actions — often without our knowledge.

D – decisions. Who gets to make decisions, and how? Are

decisions open or closed, hierarchical or collaborative, written or verbal? Decisions are an expression of power and are a critical part of culture.

These six elements are concrete and tangible. We can point to them, question them, and change them. As Meredith says, "Culture change isn't about grand gestures... it's about consistent, everyday actions."

Think of it this way: the peak gives us our direction, but it's the actions we take every day in the fields that determine whether we ever meet our aspirations. To shift culture, we need them both.

All this begs the question: how do we work together to shift culture?

Curious Questions: Set 7B

Now let's review the practical side of culture in your workplace:

- Which of the seven practical culture elements are working well in your workplace?
- Which element needs the most attention?
- What's one small action you could take to strengthen that element?

Start by making the conversation safe

Imagine trying to scale a mountain without a solid basecamp. That's what it's like trying to shift culture without first ensuring psychological safety.

Harvard professor Amy Edmondson coined the term psychological safety in 1999, defining it as "a shared belief held by members of a team that the team is safe for interpersonal risk taking."

In plain English: Do you feel safe to take risks around your team? Can you speak up, ask questions, admit mistakes, or challenge assumptions without fear of being embarrassed, rejected, or punished?

This concept hit the mainstream when Google conducted a massive internal study called Project Aristotle. They were hunting for the secret ingredients that made some teams stellar performers while others struggled. Was it a team's intellectual prowess? Was it having the right mix of personalities? Was it experience? After crunching data from hundreds of Google teams, they were surprised to learn that psychological safety was the number one factor.

Teams with high psychological safety consistently outperformed others because people weren't wasting energy on self-protection. They could focus on the work itself, not on avoiding judgment or managing impressions. When you work in a team with low psychological safety, it's like there is a second, invisible, layer of work imposed on every person.

When I work with teams, I use a simple exercise to reveal these invisible boundaries. I ask people to reflect on how safe they'd feel doing various things at work such as:

Thinking	Deciding	Disagreeing
Rethinking	Wondering	Feeling
Suggesting	Sharing	Experimenting
Enquiring	Crying	Changing
Questioning	Being ill	Thinking out loud
Learning	Challenging	Caring
Not knowing	Contributing	Admitting
Helping	Failing	Relaxing

Almost invariably, people discover they don't feel safe doing many of these things. And when we discuss who's creating these limitations, the revelation hits: there's no mysterious 'they' enforcing these rules. It's all of them. They've accidentally created these invisible boundaries for themselves.

The good news is this: if we created these invisible boundaries, we can uncreate them too.

Curious Questions: Set 7C

Now let's get personal:

- Which of the behaviours in the psychological safety section do you feel safe doing at work?
- Which behaviours feel least safe?
- Where and when could you start a discussion about this with your team?

Growing culture with questions

Once a foundation of safety exists, the real work begins: shaping the culture through curiosity. Instead of telling people what the culture is or should be, we can let it adapt through the questions we ask.

At Business Lab, the consulting firm where I was a partner, we put this questioning approach into practice by reimagining performance reviews. Research has found that these annual judgment sessions typically harm performance more than they help it.

Instead, we created what we called Progress Reviews. Rather than focusing on assessment and evaluation, these conversations were inquiry-driven and forward-looking. We asked questions like:

- What work has energised you most recently?
- Where do you feel you've made the great-est contribution?
- What would help you do even better work in the coming period?
- How might we better support your growth?

The difference was striking. Instead of dreading these conversations, we looked forward to them. Using curious questions to drive the process was far more meaningful than judging people against a set of criteria developed 12 months ago that may well have become redundant in that time.

This is just one example of letting our curiosity guide us towards a culture that worked for us. Rather than accepting the perceived wisdom ("performance reviews are necessary") we continued to question that until we found something that worked.

The anthropologist's mindset

The Culture Question asks us to become anthropologists in our own workplaces. Anthropologists immerse themselves in cultures — noticing patterns and rules without imposing judg-ment. Their primary goal is to understand *why* people do what they do.

As leaders, we can do the same. We can ask ourselves ques-tions to help us see the underlying patterns:

- Whose ideas regularly get picked up, and whose get overlooked?
- What topics make the room go quiet?
- How do people talk about mistakes?
- Which stories get told again and again?
- Where do people gather naturally, and which spaces remain empty?

By noticing these patterns without rushing to "fix" them, we gain insight into the culture we currently have — not just the one we aspire to. And only then can we take the next step on the climb. Once we see the invisible patterns, we can choose which to reinforce and which to shift.

Of course, a safe culture is only the beginning. A team can feel wonderfully comfortable and yet be stuck in groupthink. As Todd Kashdan points out in *The Art of Insubordination,* "... psychological safety reliably translates into superior performance only when sufficient minority viewpoints exist, and we permit and embrace them when present." Put simply, who's in the room matters.

That's why we'll venture into potentially uncomfortable territory in the next chapter: the gaps in our perspective we don't even know exist. Are you ready to be challenged? Let's get to it.

CHAPTER 8

The Perspectives
Question

Whose voices are missing?

"It is not our differences that divide us. It is our inability to recognize, accept, and celebrate those differences."

– **Audre Lorde**

Have you seen the racist hand dryer? A black hand goes into the slot. Nothing happens. A white hand takes its turn and — voila — it works.

The designers never meant it to be racist. But that's what happens when products, services, and systems are designed by a small subset of the world's population.

A racist hand dryer might seem inconsequential — we can survive without hand dryers — but this type of oversight is nothing short of life-threatening in other areas.

In fact, I was overwhelmed with examples when I started researching this stuff. For starters, have you heard about the impact of male crash test dummies? Females are almost twice as likely to be injured in a comparable car crash as a male — simply because most carmakers designed cars to protect the average male body. Or how about the facial recognition programmes that struggle to identify people with darker skin tones? These have led to wrongful identifications and even arrests. And don't get me started on Amazon's AI-powered recruitment tool that penalised CVs with female-oriented keywords like "women's college."

Imagine, however, if the teams behind these innovations had asked, "Whose voices are missing?" This may have led them to involving a range of people in design, testing, and implementation. What difference would that have made? How many wrongful arrests would have been avoided? How many lives might have been saved?

A diverse world needs input from diverse people. Diversity *needs* diversity.

Now, if you're bracing yourself for a lecture in this chapter, take a breath. This isn't that kind of book. I'm not here to tick a box or shame anybody. Diversity isn't just about race or gender either. It's also about how we think, the questions we ask, the blind spots we challenge, and the experiences we bring. It's about noticing what we're *not* seeing — and what might become possible when we expand our awareness.

> It's about noticing what we're not seeing — and what might become possible when we expand our awareness.

Costly shortcuts

The failure to do this can be extremely costly. In fact, the cost of missing perspectives is measured in billions of dollars even just in one industry, in one country. Research in Australia has found that poor community engagement has contributed to the cancellation, delay, or mothballing of more than $30 billion in Australian infrastructure projects over a decade, with similar pressures being seen globally. For context, that's the equivalent of about 60 to 100 hospitals — all lost because decision-makers didn't properly involve affected communities, and the resulting backlash killed the projects.

A widely cited report by McKinsey & Company found that organisations with greater gender and ethnic diversity in leadership were 21% and 33% more likely to outperform their peers. While the link isn't always causal and I'm a bit sceptical about this sort of research, the correlation speaks to something important: diversity often goes hand in hand with better decision-making and outcomes.

That's because of how our brains work. Our minds rely on subconscious biases — mental shortcuts that help us make sense of the world quickly but which often lead to limited thinking. Scientists have identified over 180 types of subconscious bias. That's a lot of mental shortcuts. That's a lot of blind spots.

The extent of these biases is quite remarkable. Harvard's Implicit Association Test, which has been taken over 26 million times since 1998, consistently shows that most people harbour unconscious biases that contradict their conscious beliefs. We think we're unbiased, but we're not. Doctors show bias in pain treatment recommendations, HR professionals show bias in CV evaluations, and judges show bias in sentencing decisions. These biases show up regardless of how fair–minded we believe ourselves to be.

These biases often go unchecked in groups where people look and think similarly. Somebody throws out an idea and everybody goes, "Yeah!" The fancy name for this is groupthink. Diverse teams are less likely to suffer from groupthink thanks to the range of different perspectives around the table.

We need to put in some extra work to make sure our systems work for more of us, more of the time.

Ultimately, this is about fairness. My life as a straight, white man has been easier in countless ways than many of my friends and colleagues. Even something as arbitrary as height affects how people are treated. Studies show taller people are more likely to be hired, promoted, and earn higher salaries compared to shorter counterparts with the same qualifications.

If you share the same sorts of privileges as me, I'm not

sharing this stuff to make us feel guilty or to downplay our achievements. I'm saying we need to put in some extra work to make sure our systems work for more of us, more of the time. By asking, "Whose voices are missing?" we take the first step toward this. It's both the smart thing and the right thing to do.

But I know from my work facilitating challenging conversations that many of us are nervous about discussions around diversity, equity, inclusion, privilege, and belonging. Even just wrapping our heads around the terms can be a challenge. With that in mind, let's start with some definitions.

So many terms, so little clarity

Have you ever found yourself smiling politely in a meeting while someone tosses around terms like "diversity," "equity," and "inclusion" — all while you're secretly thinking, "Wait, aren't those basically the same thing?"

I certainly have. And then people abbreviate them to DEI or DEIB, which sounds more like a robot from Star Wars than an important workplace concept. All this jargon can make it hard to have an honest conversation about the human experiences beneath these technical terms.

Vernā Myers, a diversity expert, explained it well in her book *Moving Diversity Forward,* "Diversity is being invited to the party; inclusion is being asked to dance."

I like this metaphor because it's something we can all picture. Let me extend it a bit:

- *Diversity is inviting lots of different people to your party.* Not just your usual friends, but people from all walks of life.
- *Inclusion is making sure everybody gets to join in.* Nobody's stuck in another room with the door locked.
- *Privilege is being the one who gets to choose the venue, decide the dress code, and pick the music.* Whether you like it or not, your choices will work better for some people than others.
- *Equity is ensuring people have what they need to enjoy the party.* It could be food, a refreshment, or a chair to sit in.
- *Belonging is when someone feels the party wouldn't be the same without them.* They're not just there to tick a box; they're a valued guest whose absence would be noticed.

These distinctions matter because the words we use shape the worlds we end up creating. A good builder knows the difference between a 'building', a 'development', and a 'dwelling'. As leaders, the words we use influence what people pay attention to and who gets to be part of the conversation.

While all these concepts have value, our journey in this chapter will focus primarily on diversity. That's because getting a mix of voices around the table is often the first step before inclusion, equity, or belonging can even begin.

Now that we've sorted out the terminology, let's explore how diversity shows up in our daily interactions — because there's more to it than what meets the eye.

Curious Questions: Set 8A

Before going any further, let's reflect on the perspectives you bring into this chapter:

- What's your view on spending time and money on diversity, equity, and inclusion? What's driving that?
- What kinds of diversity in your workplace aren't immediately visible?
- What privileges do you hold because of things outside of your control?

We're more than labels

"Hey Rose, can I ask you something?" I said to my five-year-old daughter one afternoon.

"Um, okay." She was more interested in her colouring book than my questions.

"I was wondering... how would you describe the kids in your class? How are they different from you?"

She looked up, considering the question.

"Well," she said, putting down her crayon, "Nola has black hair and Mila wears glasses. Oh! And some of them are boys!" she chuckled.

"The boys are loud," she went on, then thought better of it. "But Zifan is quiet. And Mila is super loud! Louder than the boys sometimes."

What struck me in this conversation was how she focused on what we might call 'visible diversity.' We can see or hear these differences, such as skin colour, voice tone, language, and physical traits. These often shape our initial impressions of each other.

But there's another kind of diversity that she didn't mention — the kind that develops through our experiences, like where we grow up, who we spend time with, and what happens to us. This is 'invisible diversity' that we can't absorb just by being in the same room as someone.

> How we look on the outside influences the experiences we have, which then shapes who we become.

These two types of diversity interact in interesting ways. How we look on the outside influences the experiences we have, which then shapes who we become on the inside – and vice versa.

At birthday parties, people often give my daughter dolls and my son trucks without thinking twice. Those little choices add up. My son's trucks, Hot Wheels, and Lego kits make it more likely he'll see a future for himself in engineering or construction — fields where males outnumber everybody else four to one.

Experiential Activity 8: Beyond What's Visible

Bring to mind somebody who you work with. How much do you know about what's *not* visible? Their values? Their health? Their family situation? Their experiences?

A tale of two reactions

Does talking about diversity make you uncomfortable? I recently worked with a Diversity, Equity, and Inclusion team in a government agency — helping them to make their training workshops more engaging and effective. They were finding two different reactions at their workshops. Some people shut down completely, saying almost nothing. Other people showed up with a point to prove.

I also had a leadership coaching client who once told me, "Our CEO has banned discussions about diversity because he thinks it's too divisive."

I get it. These conversations can feel like walking through a minefield — one wrong word and boom!

When discussions about diversity and privilege come up, I've noticed two common reactions that tend to derail productive conversations. I call them the Resentment Response and the Vigilance Response.

The Resentment Response often sounds like this:

- "This is just another PC/woke fad."
- "Why should I feel bad for being who I am?"
- "It's all about ticking boxes, isn't it?"
- "I believe in merit, not special treatment."
- "Hard work should be what counts."

I understand this reaction because I've felt it myself. It often comes from a place of feeling under attack — as if someone else's success must come at our expense. When someone suggests that privilege played a role in our achievements, it can feel like our efforts are being dismissed or minimised. That's understandable, even if it's not usually what's intended.

The Vigilance Response sits at the opposite end. It's like being a police officer for morality. I've experienced this as well and it's exhausting. You're on high–alert for potentially offensive comments. It often sounds like this:

- "You can't say that!"
- "How can you be so heartless?"

- "What happened to basic human decency?"
- "Maybe try educating yourself before spreading hate."
- "We're better than this as a society."

Do you identify with one reaction more than the other? Or a bit of both? It may change in different situations, depending on who you're around and what you're going through.

The problem is both responses shut down real conversation. The Resentment Response dismisses genuine concerns, while the Vigilance Response makes it a battle between good and evil, closing down the chance of a productive conversation.

What's worse is they feed off each other. Someone responds with resentment: "This is just political correctness gone mad." This prompts vigilance in others: "How can you be so insensitive?" That makes the first person dig in even deeper.

It's a vicious cycle. But surely there's a way to break it?

The third path

There is another path — one of genuine curiosity. This sounds like:

- "I don't quite get it."
- "So, you're basically saying that..."
- "Hang on, can you explain that bit again?"
- "Wait, what do you mean exactly?"

Sometimes curiosity can transform what seems like an impossible situation. In a remarkable Twitter exchange, comedian Sarah Silverman turned a troll into her biggest fan thanks to her use of empathy and curiosity. After being called a c***, she looked back at his profile and responded:

"I believe in you. I read ur timeline & I see what ur doing
& your rage is thinly veiled pain. But u know that. I know
this feeling. Ps My back ... sux too. see what happens when u
choose love. I see it in you."

The man ended up opening up about his back problem. Silverman asked her followers if anybody could help. Days later, he was thanking Silverman for her support and kindness, having received thousands of dollars in donations and in–kind medical help.

Now, I'm not suggesting we should respond to every single troll with curiosity. That places an unreasonable burden on those receiving harmful messages. My point is that approaching discussions with genuine curiosity rather than defensive judgment can open the door to much deeper understanding. This doesn't mean we have to agree, but it does mean we're listening to each other rather than just waiting for our turn to speak.

So how do we move from understanding these reactions to using curiosity to uncover missing perspectives? That's where the practical application of The Perspectives Question comes in.

When to use The Perspectives Question

The earlier we ask The Perspectives Question, the better. It's like the saying, "an ounce of prevention is worth a pound of cure."

Shortly after moving to Nelson, I heard about an example

where the question might have prevented a lot of angst. A beautiful cycleway had recently opened around the waterfront. Little did I know the project had been fraught with conflict.

My then business partner David Hammond was the acting Chief Executive of the Nelson City Council at the time. Apparently, the Council had initially selected a route without talking to the local Tāhunanui community. As a result, they managed to anger cycling advocates, local residents, and business owners all at once — a rare triple achievement!

A resolution only came after the Council formed an advisory group with members from all three of the communities they had originally isolated. Of course, by then, the delay had doubled the project's cost. All because they hadn't asked at the start: "Whose voices are we missing here?"

I've found there are four critical moments when this question can have a significant effect:

When planning a meeting: Who needs to be in the room for this discussion to be meaningful? Whose lived experience would enrich our understanding?

When designing a project: Who will be impacted by what we're creating? How might we work with them in a way that works for them?

Before making important decisions: Whose support or input will we need for this to succeed? Are we considering impacts on different communities or stakeholders — and not just the loudest ones?

During hiring processes: Are we reaching diverse candidate pools? How might our hiring practices unnecessarily limit who applies?

Fair engagement requires fair exchange

If we're going to ask people to share their perspectives, we need to make it worth their while.

Fair compensation isn't always about money (though it often should be). It can also mean genuinely listening, creating opportunities, forming real partnerships, giving credit for intellectual property, or making visible changes based on what we've heard. Without this exchange, we're extracting, not engaging.

I was reminded of this principle by Anjum Rahman, a New Zealand Muslim community leader, who told me about her experience with the National Action Plan Against Racism.

"The stories we heard during these sessions were full of trauma," she explained of the process she helped to facilitate and record.

"Many times, the participants were in tears describing things that had happened to them."

When the plan was repeatedly delayed and then watered down with a new government, Anjum felt it was a betrayal. "These people had poured their hearts out," she told me, reliving painful experiences in the hope of creating a better system.

> The lack of follow-through reinforced the very patterns of harm the process was meant to address.

The lack of follow-through reinforced the very patterns of harm the process was meant to address. There was no fair exchange: those who shared their stories of trauma had no real power in the process. They relieved their traumatic experiences — and received nothing in return. No money and no meaningful change.

This leads us to another important consideration. When we invite people to share their perspectives, especially those who are already navigating systems not designed with them in mind, we need to recognise the emotional burden we're putting on them.

First, they're already expending extra energy living in a world that doesn't work well for them. Then we ask them to educate others about these challenges and what would make things better. It's a double burden.

Before reaching out, do your homework. Research what you can without taking anyone's time. Then, if possible, find someone who can act as a guide to help you understand the context better. And when you do engage, ensure their contributions lead to meaningful action, not just more meetings.

But are you willing to change?

All of this external focus on missing perspectives is important, but there's an internal dimension that's equally crucial — and often more uncomfortable.

The Perspectives Question isn't just about who's in the room, it's also about how your presence might influence who's there.

I learned this lesson the hard way when I led an event about barriers to physical activity for young women. My gut told me I might not be the right person to lead the conversation, so I brought in a female co–facilitator. But toward the end, one adult said in front of everybody: "I don't think Paul should have been here today. I think having a man here limited the conversation."

Are you prepared to step back or step aside if that's what's needed?

Deep down, I knew she was right. Who wants to discuss periods or unwanted sexual advances in front of a man they don't know? I should have listened to my instinct and stepped away completely.

It's one thing to invite different voices to the table; it's another to adapt when their feedback challenges what we were thinking. Are you prepared to be uncomfortable? To give up some control? To step back or even step aside if that's what's needed?

Asking for diverse perspectives is tokenistic without this openness to change. People quickly sense when their input isn't truly valued, and that kind of trust, once broken, is incredibly difficult to rebuild.

Curious Questions: Set 8B

Let's think about how this applies in your work:

- When and where could you imagine yourself asking The Perspectives Question?
- When was the last time you deliberately sought out a perspective you didn't agree with?
- What's one practical step you could take this month to widen the perspectives you're hearing?

Small steps towards bigger change

Being aware of different perspectives is a start, but it's just that — a start. The Perspectives Question isn't going to single-handedly solve systemic inequities or transform our organisations overnight. But it can be the beginning of something important.

It's tempting to stay in our comfort zones, surrounding ourselves with people who share our backgrounds and viewpoints. But the most valuable insights often come from conversations that initially make us uncomfortable.

The Perspectives Question helps us take the small first step toward these uncomfortably important conversations. Each time we ask it, we're practicing a kind of intellectual humility — acknowledging that our view is incomplete and that others might see things we've missed.

When we regularly ask, "Whose voices are missing?" we start to notice patterns in our own thinking. We begin to see how our systems and processes might unintentionally exclude certain voices. We create small opportunities for change that, over time, can add up to something more significant.

CHAPTER 9

The Experience Question

What little things will make them feel big?

"I've learned that people will forget what you said, people will forget what you did, but people will never forget how you made them feel."

– Maya Angelou

There are 30 to 40 hairdressers in my town, yet every six weeks I make a beeline for Stormy's. It's not because they do better haircuts, but because of everything else. They're based in a New York–style loft with a pool table, dart board, up-to-date magazines, and even a shuffleboard table. But the moment that sealed my loyalty was when a tattooed staff member asked one afternoon, "Want a beer? It's on the house."

But why does this matter? I mean I hardly even drink beer anymore. It matters because people remember how you made them feel long after they've forgotten what you did or said. This applies whether we're leading a team meeting, designing a service, or speaking at an event — or any of the other leadership roles we perform every day.

Think about your own experiences. What makes you feel valued in a team discussion or even when you're doing something mundane like filling out an online form? It's the experience surrounding these moments that makes some mundane, some maddening, and others memorable.

People might experience our work for just minutes, but in those moments, they form a lasting impression. What matters isn't just *what* we deliver, but *how it feels* to experience it.

In the pages ahead, we'll explore how to deliberately craft these moments using The Experience Question: "What little things will make them feel big?" We'll uncover what makes some experiences stick while others fade immediately — and how to make small tweaks with big impacts on your relationships and results.

What is an experience?

We use the word experience often, but it can mean different things in different contexts. When I talk about an experience, I mean:

1. An **event**
2. That makes people **feel** something
3. And leaves a **lasting impression.**

We all create experiences, whether we're conscious of it or not. When you think about it, everything is an experience – from hiring to firing! Even something as mundane as how we format our emails becomes part of someone's experience of working with us. The question isn't whether we're creating experiences, but whether we're creating them by design or by default.

> The question isn't whether you're creating experiences — it's whether you're creating them by design or by default.

Sadly, many of us are doing the latter. Consider this tale of two invitations I received on the same day.

The first was a wedding invitation. It arrived on a carefully designed card on thick paper that directed us to a website with every detail we might need: what to wear, where to go, what gifts were appreciated, and even accommodation options for out-of-town guests.

The second was a calendar invite for what turned out to be a critical meeting with our largest client. The title simply said 'RAG Meeting' with no description — just the title. I had no idea what RAG stood for or why I needed to be there. (I later discovered we'd been trying to secure this meeting for weeks).

Two invitations; two vastly different experiences. My engaged friends understood that their invitation would set the tone for the entire wedding. My client, meanwhile, couldn't see beyond just getting something in the calendar.

Learning how to design experiences is a critical leadership skill, because everybody has high expectations these days — as customers, citizens, and employees. This isn't just a personal hunch; it turns out we have 30 years of data to back this up.

Why experiences matter now more than ever

Back in the 1990s, there was no consistent way to compare the quality of different products and services. Could you compare the quality of a car manufacturer with the quality of a restaurant franchise? Not easily, no. Could you track the quality of stuff being created across an entire country? No.

Countries had been measuring *quantity* for decades by that stage, with measures like gross domestic product (GDP). But what about *quality*? Sadly, it had been forgotten in the push for speed.

This led a bunch of economists to create something called the American Customer Service Index - a consistent way of measuring the quality of different goods and services. (Other countries soon followed suit. For instance, in New Zealand we have the Kantar Customer Leadership Index which measures customer satisfaction, reputation, and trust.)

In *The Reign of the Customer*, Claes Fornell — one of the creators of the Index — explained why it was so important. There was more global competition and services were becoming a bigger part of the economy. But most importantly, everyday people were gaining more power over companies because it was easier than ever to share information. "There was a major shift in power away from producers to consumers", explained Fornell. Today, we can share our review with a few taps and make or break an organisation's reputation.

Thanks to the Index, we now have over 30 years of data on customer satisfaction across all industries. The trend line is clear: expectations have risen, even with major disruptions like the COVID pandemic. Today, we expect more — not just as customers, but as employees, clients, and citizens. That makes it harder to stand out, and easier to disappoint. Average is no longer good enough.

So, what does this mean for how we think about experience design? What is the most important thing we can do to improve satisfaction?

Fornell has an answer for us to consider. He says it's not what most people guess: It's not better service, better quality, or lower price. Humans all differ from one another, so the most important aspect is "fit". Does your experience meet their unique needs? That's what determines their satisfaction.

But what makes an experience a 'good fit'? And why do some experiences stick with us for years while others fade immediately?

How we remember experiences

Imagine this: freezing cold water is numbing your hand. Painful seconds tick by as you grimace through the research experiment. After 60 seconds, it's finally over, and you rate the discomfort for the researchers.

Later, you undergo a similar test for 90 seconds — but with

one other difference: for the final 30 seconds, the temperature increases by just one degree from 14 to 15 degrees.

Which would you prefer to repeat? Logic says the shorter experience, right? But when psychologist Daniel Kahneman ran this famous "cold pressor" experiment, people consistently preferred the longer immersion.

We remember peaks and endings.

This counterintuitive finding revealed something important about how our brains process experiences. We don't remember events in their entirety — we remember moments, particularly the most intense peak moment and the ending.

Kahneman named this the Peak/End Rule and it governs how we evaluate everything from dental procedures to team meetings to romantic nights out.

For instance, we might forget the endless status updates from a project, but we'll never forget the moment when everything clicked during the brainstorming session — or how deflated we felt when the project just fizzled out with no acknowledgement. When we're at a conference we won't remember most of the presentations, but we'll recall the one speaker who made us cry with laughter, and whether the event ended with energy or a whimper.

Experiential Activity 9A: Peaks and Endings

Close your eyes and recall your last holiday. Give yourself 10 seconds to bring it to mind.

What was the first thing you remembered? Was it a peak moment with strong emotions? Was it the ending? Or was it something mundane?

When we understand this principle, we can stop leaving experiences to chance. Instead, we can design them with intention— shaping moments that leave a lasting, positive impression. The good news is the quality of an experience doesn't require big budgets or grand gestures. They're nice too, but often it's the small, thoughtful details that show people they matter. That's the thinking behind The Experience Question, which invites us to consider: "What little things will make them feel big?"

But knowing that small things matter is only the beginning. How do we know what little details will make the biggest impact?

Engineering powerful moments

Through years of watching what works (and what doesn't), I've found there are three key elements to consider:

Direction: Show the way

Have you ever walked into a restaurant and stood awkwardly at the entrance, unsure whether to seat yourself or wait to be shown to a table? Or sat down only to wonder whether you should order at the counter or if someone will come to you? Perhaps you're thirsty but don't know if you should help yourself to water or wait for it to be offered?

Compare that to somewhere like Subway, where clear signage walks you through each step of the process: choose your bread, your protein, your salads, your sauces. The path is laid out, allowing us to design and order a sandwich customised to our every desire in only two minutes.

These small moments of confusion may seem trivial, but they create unnecessary friction. In more serious contexts, they can also trigger anxiety too, like during an organisational restructure. Simply knowing the timeline and the steps can reduce a lot of worry. When we show people the path, they feel safer. They can focus on contributing, rather than figuring out the rules.

Showing the way is a small gesture that has an outsized impact on people's experience – and it doesn't need to be costly or fancy. It could be something as simple as a step-by-step process walkthrough. "First we'll do this, then this, then that." When people know the pathway, they can relax and enjoy the journey.

Delight: Surprise the senses

Small, unexpected delights can elevate an experience, making something stand out from the everyday routine. It's one of the easiest ways to create a 'peak' memorable moment.

There's an American tyre company that has this figured out. Nobody likes getting a flat tyre or shelling out hundreds of dollars for a replacement set. But when you pull into a Les Schwab Tire Center, an employee will drop whatever they're doing and run (yes, *run*) to your car to see how they can help.

A delightful surprise doesn't have to be big or bold.

It's a small gesture that speaks volumes. It says: you are the most important thing to us right now. Even if you know it's coming, it's still a delight to witness. It's so unlike most mechanics.

Can you say the same for how your people treat your

customers, clients, or communities? Are they running to meet them or hiding under the bonnet?

> **Experiential Activity 9B: Smiles that Spread**
>
> Let's experience a tiny moment of delight.
>
> Grab a pen (or something similar) and hold it in your mouth so it's parallel with the ground. Leave it there for 10 seconds.
>
> Do you notice how it forces a smile onto your face? How does that change your mood? Smiling is a tiny gesture that can have a massive impact.

A delightful surprise doesn't have to be big or bold. In my facilitation workshops, I sometimes include tactile resources on the tables, like playdough or colourful pipe cleaners. Many people love having something in their hands as they learn and talk, and I invariably get positive comments about these small additions, particularly from neurodiverse people who often find it hard to concentrate in dull workshops.

If you're struggling to come up with ways to create delight, just consider the senses. Could you use music to shift the mood? How might food change the experience? What might an aromatic bouquet of flowers do to people's energy? How might the placement of furniture influence the way people interact?

We all have a basic human need to be heard, understood, and celebrated.

Next time you go shopping, take note of how the store layout influences your behaviour. How different do you feel when you're in a crowded JB Hi-Fi compared to a spacious Apple store where each device is laid out like a piece of art? One feels delightful; the other feels stressful.

However, both are deliberate choices. JB Hi-Fi wants you to believe you're getting a bargain while Apple wants you to believe you're getting a premium product. Coming back to Fornell's point about fit, both companies have designed their sensory experience to match the expectations of their ideal customer.

Depth: Go deeper

We all have a basic human need to be heard, understood, and celebrated. It's why we continue to attend conferences and live events even though there's enough content on the internet for hundreds of lifetimes. We want to connect at a deeper level.

These moments of deeper connection are more important now than ever before. Professor Jarred Haar from Massey University has been tracking workplace wellbeing through his wellbeing@work surveys. Back in 2020, at the peak of the COVID lockdowns, he found that 1 in 6 people were at high risk of burnout. By April 2024, that number had climbed to an alarming 1 in 2.

Burnout isn't just being tired or grumpy. It's fighting to get out of bed in the morning. It's forgetting names and struggling with basic tasks. It's feeling like everything is beyond your capacity.

Why the dramatic increase? Professor Haar believes it's partly because we're more scared for our jobs than ever before, but it's also because we're lonely. We've designed social interaction out of our work lives even though connecting with others increases happiness.

Nicholas Epley and Juliana Schroeder at the University of Chicago discovered something fascinating about this. They asked commuters on trains and buses to either connect with a stranger or remain disconnected. Most participants expected a negative experience if they connected, but the opposite happened. Those who connected had a more positive experience than those who stayed silent. (Their research paper summed it up poignantly with the title "Mistakenly seeking solitude".)

Why, then, do we ignore each other when it feels good to connect? Epley and Schroeder suggest we underestimate other people's willingness to engage. We worry that conversations might become awkward or that we won't know how to end them. This keeps us from connecting, creating a cycle of disconnection that contributes to our collective burnout.

Experiential Activity 9C: A Little More

Take a deep breath until you simply cannot breathe any more — and then pause.

Now breathe in just a little bit more.

Notice how there was still a little extra capacity, even when you thought you were full?

We often worry about going more in depth, but we almost always have a little more capacity for listening, noticing, and connecting.

As leaders, this challenge offers an incredible opportunity. Sometimes it's as simple as starting a meeting with a thoughtful check–in question or ending a project with a moment of collective reflection to celebrate everybody's contribution.

Curious Questions: Set 9

Let's make this more concrete for you:

- Where in your work do good experiences matter the most?
- How could you more clearly show the path to the customers, clients, or citizens you serve?
- How could you delight them in some small way?
- Where could you go just a little bit deeper with them?

People who feel valued create more value

Now, to be clear, experience design isn't just about making things fun, nice, or enjoyable (although that often happens). The real purpose is to create a reciprocal loop where the quality of the experience leads to better outcomes for everybody. When we design experiences with intention, people give back with intention. It's a reciprocal exchange. When we show care, they care more. And that creates more value — for your team, your organisation, and the people you serve.

I once attended a 60-minute consultation meeting that perfectly illustrated this. It began with the government agency presenting for 45-minutes on why the unpopular government proposal was a good idea. Then they opened the floor for questions. First the local mayor stood up to speak against the proposal, followed by another local councillor. There was no room for anybody else to contribute. The only time I spoke was when someone took my email address — an address they never used for follow-up. I went home and took out my frustration on social media.

We all have an innate human need to be heard, understood, and valued. When we feel valued, we are happy to go the extra mile. When we feel overlooked, we do the opposite.

CHAPTER 10

The Conflict Question

*What's really
going on here?*

"Peace is not the absence of conflict, but the ability to cope with it."

– Mahatma Gandhi

I told you to *move that desk*!"

The words crash into me. It's 8.30am on a Monday morning and I'm sitting bleary-eyed at my desk — in need of another coffee. Last Friday, my workmate had asked me to remove a desk from our office. I'd forgotten.

Now my workmate stood in the doorway, his face flushed with anger.

He was already stressed about launching a new education programme for young men — a passion project that would eventually lead him to start his own charity. For him, the unmoved desk was the final straw in a mountain of pressure.

My reaction was instant and visceral. My throat tightened and my heart rate skyrocketed.

Without saying a word, I grabbed the desk and hauled it out like a sulking child — in flight mode. I stomped back in, threw my headphones on, let out a petulant sigh, and got back to work.

Being mature adults, we later addressed the incident as follows: we both moaned to our wives and ignored each other for two weeks!

Our collective tolerance for stress has gone out the window.

Looking back, of course, I can see that it wasn't really about the desk. My workmate was feeling the pressure of a stressful new project, and the frustration of a colleague who didn't always follow his instructions. And my childish tantrum was a cry for recognition and respect of my extra workload. But in that moment, neither of us had access to the bigger picture. We were simply caught in the drama of the conflict.

We're in a perfect storm for such conflicts. Our collective tolerance for stress has gone out the window thanks to the ongoing stress from COVID-19, increasing cost of living pressures, massive weather events, AI fear, and global political tension. Add workplace pressures like frequent staff changes, cost–cutting and restructures, and we're primed for conflict like never before.

The research confirms this. The 2023 'World Workplace Conflict and Collaboration Survey' surveyed over 5,000 full-time workers across 45 countries. Seventy percent reported the same or more workplace conflict compared to the year before.

As leaders, it's time for us all to step up. The question isn't whether we'll face conflict, but how we'll respond when it arrives. That's why The Conflict Question invites us to stay curious for a little longer by asking: "What's really going on here?" There's always something else beneath the surface — if only we can take a breath and look for it.

Experiential Activity 10A: Hard or Curious

Bring to mind an important conversation you've been avoiding or dreading.

First, take 30 seconds to imagine it being really difficult. Let your mind imagine the worst possible way it could go.

Now take 30 seconds to imagine yourself being really curious. Let your mind experience the same situation as if you were genuinely interested in the other person and everything that's happening.

Which did you find easier to imagine? How did they feel different?

Hard, courageous, or curious?

You've probably heard these moments described as hard conversations. You know what I mean, right? Giving unwanted feedback, reducing resources, changing direction, or any one of a dozen other undesirable things.

These moments make or break people. Handle them poorly, and we'll have a rush of resignations on our desk — or worse, a personal grievance claim to deal with.

But how do we have these conversations in a way that builds trust and understanding?

First, let's stop calling them hard conversations. I mean, who wants to have a difficult conversation? Not me. Not anybody, except maybe that one friend we all have who likes to argue.

That's why they got rebranded as 'brave conversations' or 'courageous conversations'. To be honest, that's not much better. What if we don't feel brave? Does that mean we're off the hook? Of course not.

No, I think we should start calling them 'curious conversations'. After all, that directs us towards the ideal stance: being interested, seeking to understand, working to listen – not just ramming our thoughts down somebody else's throats.

Almost all the outcomes we seek are on the other side of such a conversation. What conversations are you avoiding right now? And how might curiosity offer a better way in?

The sweet spot of productive conflict

Many of us tend to avoid conflict, especially in large group situations. "It all went smoothly," we celebrate. "Nobody had anything bad to say!" The absence of conflict is perceived as success.

But too little conflict is unhelpful. Have you ever been in one of those meetings where everyone just nods along? Nothing useful ever comes out of those. Without some healthy disagreement, we miss out on the magic that happens when ideas get challenged and refined.

On the flip side, when conflict gets too intense, it's like a fire alarm going off in our brains. Our nervous systems hit the panic button and we cannot think clearly; we're just trying to survive the moment.

> What we're after is that sweet spot in the middle — just enough tension to make things interesting without setting the place on fire.

What we're after is that sweet spot in the middle — just enough tension to make things interesting without setting the place on fire. It's a bit like Goldilocks and the three bears' porridge. Papa Bear's porridge was too hot; Mama Bear's was too cold; and Baby Bear's was just right.

But what constitutes the right amount? And who decides? Everybody has their own unique taste when it comes to conflict (and porridge).

Part of the answer depends on the societal norms around us. My Dutch-born friend Hester Spiegel-van den Steenhoven, author of *Thinking Big and Small*, introduced me to the idea of Dutch feedback. Open and honest disagreements are normal in Holland. There's even a name for it: the Dutch practice of 'polderen' involves negotiating and compromising to reach a consensus.

Does that sound like the norm in your workplace? Or is conflict seen as a roadblock to avoid?

> **Curious Questions: Set 10A**
>
> Here's a chance to notice how you usually think about and approach conflict:
>
> - Do you typically think of important conversations as hard, brave, or curious?
> - How comfortable are you with conflict in general?
> - What does 'unhealthy' conflict look like to you?

Beyond either/or thinking

Many of the most challenging conflicts involve what are called polarities. A polarity is an interdependent pair — two separate things that *need* each other to exist. There's no breathing out without breathing in, is there?

But let me share a real-world example from my time in the education centre I mentioned at the start of this chapter. We were part of a network of about 20 organisations across the country, all under a parent organisation.

The parent organisation was pushing for the local organisations to amalgamate into one centralised entity. Their reasoning made sense from their perspective: they saw inefficiency in having 20 different ways of doing everything and believed we could be a stronger force in a competitive market.

At the local level, though, we had serious concerns. We'd built up significant financial reserves through decades of fundraising, and it seemed wrong to send that up to a corporate head–office. We knew our community intimately and enjoyed having the freedom to create new programmes based on new needs. Did we really want to throw all that away?

The amalgamation process felt like a nasty political election. We even had secret phone calls and a couple of screaming matches!

Eventually, around 55% voted in favour of amalgamation at a tense and tightly controlled meeting. There were no cheers or celebrations, just dull relief and disappointment. Apart from the national office team, nobody seemed happy with the outcome — even those who voted in favour. We had all felt threatened and backed into a corner. *Amalgamation is good! No, it's the worst! Yes! No!*

As I reflected on the process, I realised we were grappling with some fundamental tensions that felt like either/ or choices:

- Centralisation or localisation?
- Flexibility or stability?
- Uniformity or diversity?

And yet, any good organisation needs both sides of those equations. Both centralisation *and* localisation. Flexibility *and* stability. Uniformity *and* diversity. The challenge is not to choose one side or other, but to embrace the best of them both.

This is where The Conflict Question becomes powerful. By asking, "What's this really about?" or perhaps "What else could this be about?" we open ourselves up to the other side of the story. Most conflicts aren't problems to be solved but tensions to be managed.

> **Experiential Activity 10B: Breathe and Hold**
>
> Take a deep breath and hold it in while you read.
>
> What if I asked you to never breathe out again? It would be an absurd request. But that's precisely what happens in many conflicts. In the heat of the moment, when our values are challenged, we double down on them. We subconsciously think: "I'm right, so they must be wrong ."
>
> Often we need both sides; we need to breathe in and breathe out.
>
> (Okay, you can breathe normally now!)

Yes, and...

Actors know this better than anybody. In my school days doing theatre sports, we learned the "Yes, and..." technique. The idea is simple: whatever your scene partner offers, you accept it and build upon it, rather than negating it. This doesn't mean agreeing with everything — it means accepting what's been offered and adding your own perspective.

In conflict situations, this might sound like:

- "**Yes**, I hear your concern about cost overruns, **and** I'm also thinking about the quality standards we've committed to."
- "**Yes**, centralising our operations would create efficiencies, **and** we also need to maintain our community connections."

Many of us don't give ourselves the chance to think this way. Our logical minds kick in with objections and concerns too quickly. We often default to 'Yes, but' thinking. So much so that a workshop participant once jokingly said: "If you force me to start my sentences with 'Yes, and', I'll just say 'Yes, and here are all the ways you're wrong!'"

On top of this, it's natural to miss another crucial element when we try to convince other people of our point of view: the emotional undercurrents that drive most conflicts.

Emotions are evidence

I was a real pest of a teenager. My Mum caught the brunt of it as our primary carer, but also as the only female in our home. She would get so frustrated with me and my brother's non-committal grunts, one-word sentences and messy teenage habits. But nothing would set her off quite like hearing, "Calm down, Mum."

"Don't tell me to calm down, dammit all!" she would retort, her voice thick with frustration.

Back then, I didn't get what the big deal was. I thought: Mum, you're clearly upset — so can't you just tone it down a notch?

My response was typical of a Western worldview that treats emotions as inconvenient disruptions to be managed or suppressed. You see it in the 'stiff upper lip' culture of the United Kingdom, and it shows up in lots of dismissive things we say:

- "Don't take it so personally."
- "You're overreacting."
- "Let's stick to the facts."
- "You're being unprofessional."
- "There's no need to get emotional."

The underlying message is that emotions are a problem to fix or, better yet, suppress.

But what if we've got that completely backwards? In a world where AI can do all the technical tasks to which we previously attached our identity, aren't these human emotions more important than ever before?

Nowadays, I think of emotions as bits of evidence. They're data about what matters, what's working and **Emotions spread like a contagion.** what isn't. We can ignore or downplay the signal, but that's the same as turning off a smoke alarm and ignoring the fire in our kitchen. It's nice to have the noise off, but our house is still on fire.

Social psychologists have a name for this concept: EASI Theory, short for Emotions as Social Information. The basic idea developed by Gerben van Kleef is that emotions impact the person feeling the emotion and the people around them. Whether we realise it or not, we're constantly reading and reacting to other people's emotions.

EASI Theory tells us that emotions spread through groups contagiously. One person's emotional state can shift an entire room's energy without anyone saying a word. This means we can't just ignore emotions and hope they'll go away — they'll influence everyone's behaviour whether we like it or not.

I saw this firsthand at a Ministry of Justice meeting where a senior leader arrived 30 minutes late. She huffed into the room and joined a table — clearly upset about something. Her presence immediately shifted the energy in the room. The meeting continued, but it felt awkward for quite a while. Her unacknowledged emotion shaped everyone's behaviour.

Had she simply named it, the impact would have been

contained. "Sorry everyone, I just had a tough call, but it has nothing to do with our work here." By trying to suppress her emotion, it became *more* influential, not less.

This is the paradox we face: in trying to keep emotions out of the workplace, we amplify their negative effects while losing their informational value. It's far better to acknowledge the emotion and look at what's behind it.

When I interned at a corporate law firm, I watched senior lawyers return from court in tears — only to be shuffled quickly into private offices presumably to 'pull themselves together.' Emotions were distracting; perhaps even a source of weakness. But what if those tears contained valuable information about a client's needs, the sustainability of workloads, or the support systems needed?

The Conflict Question invites us to treat emotions as valuable data rather than inconvenient disruptions. Instead of dismissing feelings as overreactions, they give us an opportunity to learn more about what matters.

But emotions aren't the only thing we need to decode. The way people express conflict itself follows distinct patterns that, once recognised, can improve how we respond.

Curious Questions: Set 10B

Before we look at the different faces of conflict, let's reflect on your emotional intelligence:

- How easy is it for you to see the other side of an argument?
- How acceptable is it to display strong emotions in your workplace?
- Where do your views on the role of emotions at work come from?

The four faces of conflict

"I can't believe you're suggesting that!"

Marco, known for his passionate advocacy, is on his feet, hands gesturing emphatically.

Jane's response is immediate: her shoulders tense and her voice becomes ice cold. "Well, if you actually looked at the data for once..."

Meanwhile, Priya is surreptitiously taking notes, sinking into her chair and refusing eye contact.

All the while, Tom has his arms folded with a seen-it-all-before expression that clearly communicates, "This again? What a waste of time."

It's an imagined moment, but it captures four common conflict responses I see in teams all the time.

Most of us, when we think about conflict, picture somebody like Marco: loud and confrontational. But conflict doesn't always sound like shouting. Sometimes it hides in certainty, silence, or a raised eyebrow.

Let's explore this further through these four conflict personas. They're a simplification of the richness of different behaviours that show up in conflict. But simplifying them can help us respond more effectively in conflict.

- **The Activist** is values-driven and outspoken. Like Marco, they speak up when something feels morally or emotionally important.
- **The Expert is** evidence-led and sharp. Like Jane, they come armed with facts and credibility, aiming to correct or clarify.

- **The Observer** is thoughtful and reserved. Like Priya, they appear to withdraw during conflict, often reflecting deeply before speaking (if at all).
- **The Sceptic** is cautious and experienced. Like Tom, they've seen many things fail and resist being swept up in enthusiasm again.

The first time I introduced these at a conference, somebody goes: "Oh, I'm all of those!" And that's so true: we can all play different roles in different contexts.

They're all valuable

It's important to say that none of these personas is inherently bad or better. Each response brings value in different ways.

Activists connect us to values. They help us to see when something important has been overlooked or downtrodden. At the same time, their passion can be misread as aggression or inflexibility. In response, try to acknowledge the underlying value rather than dismissing their response as emotional or over-the-top.

Experts bring evidence and rigour. They're valuable because they've read the reports and done the research. At the same time, their certainty can crowd out other experiences. In response, try to honour their knowledge before inviting others to contribute.

Observers bring perspective. They often see the bigger picture while others are lost in the weeds, but they risk being sidelined or overlooked. In response, try to bring them into the conversation or speak to them one-on-one.

Sceptics bring caution. They help us avoid past mistakes by reminding us of the risks. At the same time, their protective instincts can stifle new ideas – or simply a better attempt at an old idea. In response, invite them to consider how things could be different this time.

I find it fascinating to observe how these personas interact. When an activist preaches about an underlying value, experts often feel the need to push back with data. Or when an observer goes quiet, an activist may interpret this as a sign of disinterest — when it's the complete opposite.

My point here is not for you to try and place people into these boxes, but simply to acknowledge that conflict shows up in multiple ways. Once we're able to recognise these patterns, we can approach conflict with more curiosity than defensiveness. It's like putting on a new pair of glasses — suddenly we can see clearly what was previously a blur of emotional reactions.

Curious Questions: Set 10C

Let's think about how you typically show up in conflict:

- If someone got angry or frustrated in front of you, how would you typically respond?
- Which of the four conflict personalities do you most often exhibit? Activist, expert, observer, or sceptic?
- Which type do you find most challenging to respond to — and why?

Curiosity cures animosity

In a world increasingly characterised by polarisation and tribalism, the ability to sit with conflict and consider, "What's this really about?" is more valuable than ever. Curious conversations won't be easy, but they give us a chance to bridge divides and change the dynamics of teams, organisations, and communities. We become like diplomats who understand that in most disputes, everyone has valid reasons for thinking, feeling, and acting the way they do.

The Conflict Question points us towards that diplomatic superpower. Instead of getting stuck in "I'm right, you're wrong" thinking, the question nudges us towards the deeper meaning behind a surface–level disagreement.

I wonder how the question might have changed the desk incident at the start of this chapter – if either of us had paused to consider what was going on under the surface? We might have been able to talk with each other, rather than endure several days of uncomfortable silence.

CHAPTER 11

The Learning
Question

*What's a small and
safe way to test that?*

"Not everything that can
be counted counts, and not
everything that counts can
be counted."

– William Bruce Cameron

As a bright-eyed graduate, I joined the Ministry of Justice to find massive charts lining the walls of our office.

"What are those?" I asked, curious.

"They're the court waiting times," my manager explained. "Our goal is to halve the time people have to wait to get their cases resolved."

It was a worthy goal, given that average waiting times for some courts stretched beyond two years. As the saying goes: justice delayed is justice denied.

At first, the 50% faster target seemed effective. We saw quick improvements as people rallied around the target.

But soon, it became more challenging to reduce the waiting times, and I started to notice some questionable behaviours. Immense effort was invested into a handful of cases that would drastically improve our stats. I hate to think how much money was spent hunting through records for anomalies — anything to shave days off the average waiting times. Every team was expected to contribute to the goal, even though many had little or nothing to do with court waiting times.

Eventually, it seemed we'd lost sight of the goal's real purpose — making the court system fairer and faster. The aim was to hit the target. It didn't matter how.

I didn't realise it at the time, but the experience was teaching me an important leadership lesson: when we focus too much on hitting numbers, we often forget why we started counting in the first place.

The target trap

Conventional wisdom tells us that objectives, goals, and targets are essential. We must keep score, right? This way of thinking shows up everywhere. Politicians set targets for improving hospital waiting times. CEOs set 'big hairy audacious goals' to guide their entire organisation. We point to these targets with pride. Don't worry, we seem to be saying, we've got things figured out.

Targets can backfire, creating unexpected consequences.

But targets can backfire, creating unexpected problems — especially in a world changing as rapidly as ours.

For starters, they often encourage short-term thinking. Long-term thinking fades into the background when success is measured by immediate results. In our race to chase quick wins, we often end up solving surface level issues rather than addressing the underlying causes.

This is what happened with the Ministry's 50% faster target. It became a textbook example of economist Charles Goodhart's law: "When a measure becomes a target, it ceases to be a good measure." Our obsession with hitting the target meant the metric soon lost its value as a genuine indicator of progress.

Numbers can lie

To make sense of this challenge, I spoke to Toby Lowe, the lead voice behind the 'Human Learning Systems' approach to public service in the United Kingdom. He told me a story that mirrored my own experience. As a charity CEO, he was asked by a funder to fudge their outcomes data — not out of malice, but because the system left no other option. As Toby told me:

"He was just like, 'No, I want to give you this money, but I'm constrained by this kind of outcomes-based form... just write *this here* and write *this here* and write *this here.*' And I'm like, 'But that's not true.'"

For Toby, that was the moment he realised people were making decisions based off data they couldn't trust. Good people were gaming the system because hitting the target mattered more than telling the truth.

He went on to put it bluntly: "[We] are operating off a set of data that's kind of made up...[We've] created a system where everyone systematically lies."

When we become so focused on hitting metrics, it's easy to lose sight of the bigger picture. The work becomes about improving the metric, regardless of what might be happening in the real world.

In short, when targets take over, we turn off the very thing that makes humans unique — our capacity to learn and adapt. So how do we break free from this pattern?

Curious Questions: Set 11A

Let's consider how targets and numbers impact your workplace:

- What numbers are most commonly tracked in your workplace?
- How does tracking those numbers influence decisions and actions?
- Where (if at all) have you noticed targets having unwanted effects?

Managing learning, not outcomes

Toby's advice was to shift the focus of our role as leaders. At its core, I see this as a shift from managing outcomes to managing learning.

	Managing Outcomes	Managing Learning
Aim	Hitting the target	Getting better
Suits	Simple situations	Complex situations
Uses	Targets to measure success	Feedback and reflection to guide progress
Asks	*"How do we improve our numbers?"*	*"What are our numbers teaching us?"*

Managing outcomes is the typical way of doing things. We set clear targets, measure progress against them and hold people accountable for hitting their numbers. But there's a tonne of evidence showing how futile this is. We cannot prove our actions *caused* an outcome in a complex system, just as we can't claim that throwing a stone in the ocean causes a wave across the sea. Maybe it contributes; maybe it doesn't.

Toby often uses the example of reducing obesity rates to illustrate the point. He found over 100 variables that could influence somebody's eating and exercise behaviours — your friends, your hobbies, your job, your commute, your social media, and so on.

We can influence outcomes, but we cannot control them.

If you were providing a weight loss programme, how could you confidently pick out your programme's impact from all those other factors? Somebody might have changed jobs, TV shows, or friends — or experienced any other number of events that influenced their eating and exercise. How would you know exactly what impact your programme had? At best, you could make a hopeful guess.

It's the same for any complex issue. Whether you're trying to reduce waiting times or increase customer satisfaction, we can't *control* those outcomes. We can influence them, but we can't control them. There are simply too many variables at play.

Managing learning is much more useful — mainly because it's *actually* possible. We do this by making it easier for people to learn about what's working, and then do more of that. This means creating the conditions where good learning can happen — bringing the right people together, providing time for reflection, removing barriers that prevent experimentation, and ensuring people can adapt based on what they find.

This doesn't mean we're ignoring data and metrics; it means using them for a different purpose. Instead of asking "How do we improve our numbers?" we're asking, "What are our numbers teaching us?" Ironically, the outcomes we care about are more likely to emerge from this learning approach, but they come from good learning rather than direct control.

Small steps toward bigger change

The Learning Question is a simple but powerful way of shifting us towards a learning approach by asking: "What's a small and safe way to test that?"

This approach aligns with what entrepreneur Reid Hoffman calls 'taking small risks to address big risks.' I first heard him talk about this in his now-famous Bologna Business School commencement address about AI. Hoffman was explaining that his optimism about AI stemmed from the fact that humans are tweaking it, bit-by-bit, release-by-release – taking lots of small risks to offset the much larger risks of AI going rogue on us all. Only time will tell whether the theory rings true in that context, but the theory remains useful all the same.

Small risks insulate us from bigger risks.

As a founder of LinkedIn and an experienced investor, Hoffman's point is that the biggest dangers often come from failing to adapt to changing conditions. By taking small, calculated risks and learning from what happens, we can reduce the much larger risk of becoming obsolete or ineffective as things change.

This approach works because it fundamentally changes the risk equation. By testing ideas at a small scale first, we avoid the major failures that could derail our efforts entirely. Think of it like dipping your toe in the water before diving into the deep end.

There's a psychological benefit too. Small experiments feel less threatening than sweeping changes, helping people to adopt new approaches. Typically, there's less resistance when someone suggests a pilot programme rather than a complete system overhaul.

Perhaps most importantly, The Learning Question accelerates our learning cycle. Multiple small tests provide far more learning opportunities than a single big implementation. Each experiment teaches us something, and those lessons compound over time.

The Lifehack story

My first experience of this learning approach came when I joined Lifehack, an initiative aimed at improving youth mental health in New Zealand where our youth suicide statistics are among the worst in the world.

Lifehack originally launched with a series of weekend hackathon events, bringing together young people to create technology solutions for mental health.

Despite initial enthusiasm, most of the projects fizzled out within a year.

The young participants were juggling transitions from school to work or further study, and developing long–term solutions for such a complex issue was overwhelming. The hackathon format, while stimulating, bred a fear of failure. Success was narrowly defined as whether the app or project took off immediately, so participants felt pressured to produce results rather than learn and grow. In other words, it was a Managing Outcomes approach.

Lifehack's breakthrough came when they set an experiment based on this question: "What if, instead of incubating ideas, we incubated people?" This was a fundamental question that looked under the surface at their most basic assumptions about how change happens.

Ironically, by focusing on what people needed, their projects flourished — with initiatives like Shift, an award–winning organisation focused on improving young women's wellbeing, and Mindfulness for Change, a leadership community using the science of mindfulness to improve social outcomes.

I joined the Lifehack team during this shift and I was impressed with how they used experimentation to guide their work. They'd identify an assumption, design a small experiment, and document what they learned. This disciplined approach to learning became a cornerstone of Lifehack's impact. Each experiment built upon the previous one, creating a web of insights that informed their work. Their disciplined experimentation turned the abstract concept of 'learning' into something much more concrete.

Learning at scale with The Construction Accord

But could this approach work at a much larger scale, with higher stakes and more complexity?

To understand this, a few years later I spoke with Judy Zhang, Director of the Construction Accord — a partnership between government and industry to transform one of New Zealand most challenging sectors.

When Judy became Director of the Construction Accord, she inherited a gnarly challenge. The construction sector employs over 280,000 people and is critical for New Zealand's wellbeing. We all need a dry and healthy home. But the industry is also plagued by systemic issues like workforce gaps, poor contracting practices, and what Judy diplomatically called "behavioral aspects of how the sector works amongst themselves."

Traditional outcomes–based approaches would have focused on setting targets and monitoring compliance. Instead, the Accord set out to use a learning approach.

Rather than having a separate evaluation team, everyone on the Accord team was tasked with playing a role in evaluation and learning. As Judy put it: "We should all be curious about how things are progressing."

My conversation with Judy was only a few years into the Accord's lifetime, so it was too early to pinpoint its long–term outcomes. But they've created solutions that wouldn't have emerged from top–down planning — like guidance on plasterboard alternatives that helped councils and businesses get through supply shortages without requiring regulatory change.

"This is about transformation for industry," Judy told me, "and often we can't catch every single person to be involved in design or even the delivery, but how do we ensure that we have those that are willing as well as those that can challenge us in the right conversations?"

That last part is important. A learning approach requires us not just to be open to challenge, but to create the conditions for it. This brings us nicely to some concerns you might have about how realistic this approach is in the real world of reporting to boards, funders, and shareholders who expect you to deliver results — and fast.

Yeah, but...

In my experience, the biggest challenge with managing earning is getting the permission we need to put this approach into practice. In a world that's focused on delivering results, some people might see a learning approach as a bit of a cop-out.

Let's explore two common concerns you'll need to work with.

"But we're accountable for results"

My workmate Penny Hagen experienced this challenge firsthand at Lifehack. Penny was an outstanding researcher and she wrote insightful reports showing what we were learning from our experiments. But the bigger challenge was explaining our learning-based approach to our primary funder, the Ministry of Social Development.

When Lifehack was established, the Ministry set targets such as the number of young people involved in events. As Lifehack's model shifted from working directly with young people on apps to working with adults–who–work–with–young–people, our stats looked much worse on paper — even though we were making a much bigger impact.

> We were succeeding in ways our original metrics couldn't capture.

This is the Target Trap in action. The numbers suggested we were failing when we were succeeding in ways our original metrics couldn't capture.

So, what can we do if we want to prioritise learning, but we're being held accountable for results we cannot control? The solution isn't to abandon accountability but to be accountable for learning. Instead of "We reached 500 young people," it might become "We discovered that training youth workers reaches 10x more young people than direct programmes, so we've shifted our approach accordingly." It's a different flavour of accountability, but it's accountability nonetheless.

"But what if the experiment fails and we look bad?"

This is another big concern, particularly if you're working in a political environment where even small failures can risk a front–page blow–out. As Judy from the Construction Accord said to me:

> "There's always a temptation to sweep things under the carpet when they haven't quite gone according to plan, because there's public money being spent. With a learning approach, you're always trying to figure out why things have happened and how you can improve, and that does mean sometimes shining a light on things that haven't quite gone according to how you hoped they would."

The appetite for visible experimentation can be limited in environments where Ministers, board members, journalists, community members, or shareholders are demanding quick results.

To combat this, we can refocus people on the cost of *never* experimenting. The real risk is gradual decline, missed opportunities, and eventual irrelevance. These far outweigh the risk of small, well–communicated experiments. A standup comedian would never test her new material in the Netflix special on opening night. She would test it in lots of small comedy clubs, refining each joke week after week. We must do the same.

Curious Questions: Set 11B

Now let's think about the role learning plays in your workplace:

- What's at risk if your workplace doesn't adapt and learn quickly enough?
- To what extent are you managing the process of learning in your workplace right now?
- What barriers might you face if you shifted from managing outcomes to managing learning?

Becoming scientists in our work

The Learning Question invites us to think like a scientist. Not in a lab coat kind of way, but with a mindset of curiosity and openness.

Instead of sticking to rigid plans, we try something, see what happens, and adjust. When things don't go as expected, it's not failure but feedback. That shift alone can reduce the fear of getting it wrong and help us make faster progress.

It's not about ditching accountability, but about being accountable to learning. It takes a different kind of discipline to pay attention to what's emerging and act on it.

That's not to say this will be easy. You'll find that some people see this approach as a bit loose or soft. In my experience, it's much more rigorous. It's easier to hit arbitrary targets than to stay present with the messy reality of the world. But it's this learning process where real progress happens.

After all, that's what we're after with The Question Effect. As leaders, we're not asking questions purely for curiosity's sake; we're asking them to lead us to the real issues rather than wasting time, money, and energy on surface-level problems.

This brings us to the end of our exploration of Leading Questions in Part 2. We've seen how certain questions can dramatically change how people think, feel, and act. But it's not just the words themselves that do that, is it? What about all the other things at play, like the environment, the people, and the context?

We can't control all those factors, and we don't need to. But there are two important areas that we can influence to increase our impact and reduce our stress. That's where we turn now in Part 3, as we look beyond the content of our questions to explore the conditions that make questions powerful in the first place.

Part 3

SETTING THE STAGE FOR QUESTIONS

CHAPTER 12

Framing

Frames trump facts

"Unfortunately, simplistic framing of problems leads to simplistic answers."

– **Mariana Mazzucato**

D o you remember the early days of COVID-19? In March 2020, I was sitting in my living room watching our Prime Minister address the nation. Her voice was calm but firm as she announced unprecedented restrictions on our day-to-day freedoms.

"We must act now to save lives," she said, explaining that we were moving to Alert Level 4. Schools and businesses were to close their doors. We would all stay home except for essential trips.

And remarkably, we did just that.

We stayed off the streets, formed our bubbles and started doing those weird Zoom quiz nights with friends we hadn't spoken to in years. We queued outside supermarkets, obediently standing two metres apart.

Compliance was extraordinarily high, despite the extremity of the restrictions. But why? I believe it was largely due to the government's presentation of the public health crisis — what we might call its 'framing'. The lockdowns were about saving people's lives.

But as the weeks turned into months, competing frames began to emerge. 'What about the economy?' business leaders asked. 'What about mental health?' others wondered. 'What about personal freedom?' questioned still more. The public health measures didn't fundamentally change, but how we thought about them did.

The context controls the conversation

The same dynamic plays out in our workplaces every day, albeit with lower stakes than a global pandemic. "Frames trump facts" said cognitive linguist George Lakoff in his 2004 book *Don't Think of an Elephant*. Once a frame is established, it shapes how every subsequent question and point is heard. Our framing determines whether people see a project meeting as a tick-box exercise or a meaningful opportunity to make a difference. It determines whether our workmate hears criticism or constructive feedback in a one-on-one conversation.

Framing sets the stage for everything that follows. As my mentor Matt Church, author of 20 leadership books, would often say: "If you control the context, you control the conversation."

Throughout this book, we've been exploring the power of The Question Effect to create better outcomes. But a question only works if it lands in the right soil. Framing is how we prepare that soil. It's how we create the conditions for curiosity and engagement.

In this chapter, we'll explore seven powerful framing devices which we can use to set the stage for any important conversation – whether it be a team offsite, a restructure, an opinion article, a speech, a one-to-one meeting, or any other leadership communication. But what is framing exactly? Let's begin by exploring a simple metaphor that makes this abstract concept tangible.

What is framing?

Picture yourself dumping out a fresh jigsaw puzzle. What's your first move? If you're like most people, you don't dive straight into the middle of that sky-blue section. No way. You hunt for those distinctive corner pieces and connect them with the straight edges until you've built a complete frame.

It's only then that the chaos starts to make sense. That random piece with the bit of red flower suddenly has a home. The frame boxes things in and turns a pile of disconnected pieces into a solvable challenge.

In leadership, framing does the same thing – but with our words.

A frame is the context we set around an issue. It's "the ability to paint a picture with words," says Gail Fairhurst, a communication professor who's spent her career studying framing. In her book *The Power of Framing: Creating the Language of Leadership*, she argues that the primary work of leadership involves "managing meaning through framing." When we don't do this, we leave a big hole which people quickly fill with rumours, anxiety, or assumptions.

Without a strong framing, we feel lost.

Personally, I think framing is the most underrated leadership tool. Without a strong framing, people feel lost, just as you would be if you tried to complete a puzzle without the box or any edge pieces.

Experiential Activity 12: The Power of Framing

You can experience the power of framing for yourself right now. (I learned this trick from Martha Ronk, an American-born English professor.)

Hold up your fingers in a rectangle, with your thumbs touching your forefingers. Put the frame right in front of your eyes. Now close one eye and move your attention around the room. Can you see how the frame changes how you perceive the room?

Frame, frame, and frame

Many of us skip framing without even realising it. We assume everyone sees what we see. After all, isn't the picture on the box obvious? But as leaders, we might have been staring at that box for months or years. We've forgotten what it's like to see the pieces *without* knowing what they create. Economists call this the 'curse of knowledge.' Once we know something, it's nearly impossible to remember what it was like *not* to know it. As Ralph Waldo Emmerson once said: "The mind, once stretched by a new idea, never returns to its original dimensions." We forget that others haven't attended the same meetings, read the same reports, or had those illuminating hallway conversations that shaped our understanding.

That's why framing is never a 'once and done' thing. Our real-world contexts are constantly shifting. As leaders, we must continually reset the frame. Context shifts like sand under our feet. Even within a single conversation, the frame that worked for opening remarks might need refreshing before tackling a thorny decision.

The same is true with a jigsaw puzzle: we don't look at the box once, commit it to memory, and put it back on the shelf. We're continually stealing the box from our fellow puzzle enthusiasts to check where the next piece might go. Regular, intentional reframing — sometimes as simple as saying 'Remember we're here for...' — keeps questions firmly rooted in fertile ground.

Now that we understand what framing is and why it matters, the next logical question is: how do we do it?

Curious Questions: Set 12A

Before we look at the framing devices, let's consider why this matters:

- Where do you see framing being most relevant for you: in team offsites, restructures, opinion articles, speeches, meetings — or somewhere else?
- What's the risk for you if you frame poorly in that context?

How to frame

There are countless ways to frame a question or curious conversation. Even just saying "I'm curious" before asking a question is a simple framing device that changes how people hear your question.

As I was writing this chapter, my list of framing devices soon ballooned to 20 or more, which was far too overwhelming. I've condensed that list down to seven devices that give us the best chance of sparking The Question Effect. We can use these in any leadership context where we want to set the scene for a curious and impactful discussion. No one device is better than the other, and sometimes it may help to use a combination.

Frame	Role	Action	Outcome
Purpose	Orient	Tell us why	Sets direction
Contrast	Redirect	Tell us what it's not	Disrupts the default
Enemy	Rally	Name the villain	Creates camaraderie
Metaphor	Translate	Tell us what it's like	Makes it stick
Mitigation	Disarm	Name it to tame it	Builds trust
Model	Organise	Make it visual	Simplifies ideas
Place	Signal	Change the space	Normalises behaviour

You've probably seen them all at some stage: on the news, in political debates, on social media, in conversations, or in training workshops. Learning about them might feel like learning a magician's secret tricks. You may even feel a bit deflated as you start to see how frames have been used to manipulate you in the past. That's the thing about framing: it's powerful. Like any powerful tool, we must use it ethically and not to manipulate others for personal gain.

Curious Questions: Set 12B

Let's explore your thoughts on those framing devices:
- Which of those seven framing devices were new to you?
- Which device would you like to use more deliberately?

Tell us why – the purpose frame

Let's start with the most foundational framing device. When our purpose is clear, even difficult questions find receptive ears. When it's fuzzy or missing, even brilliant questions fall flat.

When I teach people the purpose frame in my leadership programmes, I simply invite them to ask each other: 'Why are we here?' It sounds basic, but this little question packs a surprising punch. Many of us understand our purpose deep down but struggle to explain it out loud when pressed.

For instance, consider this question: What's the purpose of a weekly team meeting? Is it to connect? To share information? To get on the same page? These are the answers that people give when I pose this question in training workshops. But none of those three things are purposes.

One of my first mentors, Tom Watkins, explained this to me years ago. "There's a difference between purpose and process," he told me. "Process is *what* you're doing; purpose is *why* you're doing it." The purpose of a team meeting could be many things: to make us a high-performing team, to ensure we learn as fast as possible, to reduce wasted time during the week – and so on. These are reasons why we would meet, not just things we would do while we meet.

Make it positive, not negative

One common trap when trying to explain our purpose is to make it about a problem. I get why this happens. Problems demand our immediate attention, and we love to solve them. But it's far more powerful to frame a purpose around an aspiration. Research by public narrative specialists at *The Workshop* explains why this matters. When we frame around a problem, we put people in a negative state of mind, making them critical rather than collaborative.

Consider these two ways of framing the same issue:

- 'We need to end homelessness in our city' (problem-based)
- 'Everyone deserves a warm, dry place to sleep at night' (aspiration-based).

The problem-based purpose raises doubts in our mind. Is it even possible to end homelessness? How could we do that? How much would that cost?

The aspiration-based purpose connects to fundamental values like kindness and fairness. Who could disagree with the statement that everybody deserves a warm, dry place to sleep at night?

Daniel Kahneman and Amos Tversky famously demonstrated the importance of positive framing in a 1981 study dubbed the "Asian disease problem".

Imagine you're faced with this tough decision. A new disease is expected to kill 600 people, and you must choose between several policy options.

- Half of the participants saw one option framed as "200 lives will be saved."
- The other half saw the same option framed as "400 people will die."

Which sounds worse to you? Or have you noticed they're both the same?

What the researchers found was that 72% of people chose the positive "lives saved" frame while only 22% chose the same option when it was framed as "400 lives lost".

And it makes sense, right? While both are the same outcome, they *feel* completely different.

We can apply this to all sorts of leadership challenges. Think of a restructure, for instance. Some are framed as "cutting costs" (a negative or problem-based purpose) while others are framed as "reshaping for growth" (a positive aspirational purpose). One evokes pessimism; the other evokes optimism.

While a problem-based purpose asks, 'What bad thing could go away if we did this?' an aspirational purpose asks, 'What good could we achieve if we did this?' This small tweak has a massive impact.

Make it tangible

The second challenge with purpose frames is not sounding like a jargon-factory. Too often, I hear people describing their purpose with vague corporate-speak: 'We need to complete the stakeholder engagement mapping for our Strategic Delivery Framework.' Um, excuse me?

A purpose should be clear and tangible. If we were to say it to my kids, they should understand it. 'We need to figure out who cares about this project so we know who to work with this year.' This is saying the same thing as the jargon-version, but you can almost see, touch, and feel the purpose. Anyone hearing this would better understand why this stuff matters.

We can take this a step further by giving our aspiration a currency. In essence, there are three main currencies of value: time, money, and happiness.

- **Time:** Will your purpose save time or give people more time for the things that matter?
- **Money:** Will your purpose make or save money?
- **Happiness:** Will your purpose help people feel good — whether physically, emotionally, or socially?

Connecting to these currencies forces us to explain our purpose in much simpler language.

For instance, here's a typical jargon-heavy purpose statement for a software project: 'Our purpose is to implement an enterprise-grade, cloud-based solution that enables cross-functional collaboration and workflow optimisation.'

But what if we connected that to the three currencies?

- We'd like to save you 5 hours every week on emails and meetings (time),
- reduce an estimated $4,000,000 per year in project delays (money),
- and eliminate those frustrating miscommunications that make us all want to tear our hair out (happiness).

Can you see how this makes it concrete and real? It feels relevant to people's daily experiences, not just to an organisation's bigger objectives.

Framing around a shared aspirational purpose might sound obvious, but it's at the core of every powerful frame. The next framing devices can then help us to bring that frame to life much faster and more vividly.

Tell us what it's not – the contrast frame

Have you seen the 1993 courtroom drama film *Philadelphia*? Denzel Washington plays Joe Miller, a lawyer representing Andrew Beckett, a man wrongfully dismissed from his law firm after being diagnosed with AIDS. In one of the film's most powerful courtroom scenes, Miller uses a clever framing device:

> *"...this case is not just about AIDS, is it? So let's talk about what this case is really all about: the general public's hatred, our loathing, our fear of homosexuals and how that climate*

*of hatred and fear translated into the firing of this particular
homosexual, my client, Andrew Beckett."*

Can you spot the contrast frame? Denzel Washington's
character acknowledges the dominant story and then provides
a different one. He's saying: stop obsessing about the disease
and focus on justice.

The structure for a contrast frame is simple. It's basically:
"You might think this is about X. But it's really about Y."

A contrast frame disrupts the default way of thinking. They
work best when there's a dominant story already taking up
space. Is there a dominant narrative in your workplace? What
if you accepted that story – and then built a new one on top
of it?

Name it to tame it – the mitigation frame

Most of us are sceptical about anything that seems too good
to be true. We've all heard people talk a big game and fail to
deliver. We've all had bad experiences as customers, clients,
and citizens.

This is why the mitigation frame is so important. By
acknowledging people's concerns, they seem less concerning.
When we avoid people's concerns, they suspect we have something to hide.

I first spotted this technique in advertising. There's a simple
formula used for social media ads that goes like this:

- **Achieve [good thing]:** This is the core benefit, usually
  tied to time, money, or happiness as we explored in the
  purpose frame above.
- **Without [bad thing]:** This is something we've previously experienced and want to avoid at all costs.

- **Even if [tough thing]:** This is something we're worried will get in the way of what we want.

For example, let's pull that into an advertisement for our imaginary new software system.

- This system will help us deliver projects in half the time and budget [good thing],
- without a 12 month onboarding cycle [bad thing],
- even though lots of us aren't great with technology [tough thing].

This formula works because it directly addresses what people care about while acknowledging past pain points. It's a one-two punch of empathy and credibility.

You've probably seen this framing device used in political speeches as well. A candidate might say something like: "I know you're worried about the cost of living. And you've lost faith in politicians who've let you down in the past." Statements like these make us feel heard and understood.

When we name a concern, we tame that concern.

The power of the mitigation frame is due to a simple psychological principle: when we *name* a concern, we *tame* that concern.

Dr Dan Siegal coined this phrase in his psychiatry research at the UCLA School of Medicine. He and his team conducted a series of brain scans that showed how naming an emotion reduced activity in the amygdala (our stress centre) and increased activity in the pre-frontal lobe (our logical centre). Even saying something as simple as "I feel bad" had that effect.

That's the power of the mitigation frame. When we name it, we tame it.

Tell us what it's like – the metaphor frame

Metaphors are often called "word pictures" — and for good reason. They convey a huge amount of meaning in just a few words. When we tie an idea to a metaphor, we connect it to a whole body of meaning already existing in somebody's mind.

(By the way, let's not worry about the differences between metaphors, similes and analogies. For our purposes, they all do the same job.)

I recently saw a striking example of a metaphor frame following one of the biggest rain events in New Zealand's history. Political commentator Matthew Hooten wrote an opinion piece entitled: "It's too late to avoid climate change – now we have to adapt".

Sustainability expert Carolyn Mortland responded with a brilliant counter-metaphor:

> *When your plumbing springs a leak, do you choose to either turn off the water OR mop the floor?*
> *The inconvenient truth is we need to do both.*

In a few short words, she reframes the issue by connecting it to something we can all picture. Nobody would start mopping the floor with the water still pouring in. The metaphor does a lot of heavy lifting to change our perspective about this complex issue.

This is the power of a metaphor frame. It's a translation device that helps people to understand something complex – and remember it for weeks afterwards.

Embrace the enemy — the villain frame

Nothing motivates like a common enemy. I don't mean blaming individuals, but naming a system, idea, or story that's getting in the way of what matters. When we name a villain, we're subtly casting the rest of us as the heroes.

Psychologists Henri Tajfel and John Turner uncovered the mechanics behind this device back in 1979. Tajfel was a Polish-born Jewish Holocaust survivor and he wanted to understand how ordinary people could commit such atrocious acts. In their most famous study, they assigned teenage boys to two meaningless groups — supposedly based on whether they preferred the paintings of Klee or Kandinsky, two abstract artists. In reality, the groups were random. The boys didn't know each other and had no reason to identify with their group.

Yet when the researchers asked the boys to anonymously allocate money to other boys, they consistently gave more money to people in their own group. And even more than that, many even chose to give less to everyone overall, just to create a bigger gap between the two groups.

Name a threat to unify a group. Us-and-them thinking is frighteningly easy to trigger, and scarily powerful. You see this framing device in politics all the time. Right-leaning politicians villainise red-tape restrictions, the elitist media, lazy immigrants, and greedy tax-and-spend politicians. Meanwhile, left-leaning politicians villainise fat cat corporate leaders, the exploitative 1%, and fossil fuel giants. The psychology is the same: name a threat to unify a group.

As leaders, we must tread carefully with the villain frame. Feel free to villainise broken systems or outdated mandates, but never people. For instance, we could villainise:

- Short-term thinking that sacrifices long-term value
- Analysis paralysis that delays action
- Risk aversion that stifles growth

- Complacency that breeds mediocrity
- Micromanagement that stifles autonomy.

I could go on and on! We can then bring the villain to life. Give it a name, tell us its origin story, explain how it has served us — and then call us to set it aside.

The villain frame is powerful. Like anything powerful, it needs a careful hand. Use it to unify, but never to divide.

Draw it out – the model frame

This framing device might be my favourite – mainly because I love drawing diagrams in workshops. Any time we sketch a venn diagram, triangle, or 2x2 matrix, we're framing. A good visual model shapes how people think by showing the relationships between ideas. They act like a lens, bringing certain things into sharp focus while blurring out others.

To see this in action, let's take one of the most well-known of them all: the Project Management Triangle.

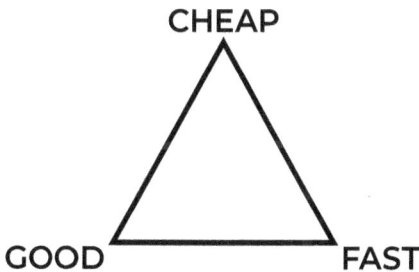

CHEAP

GOOD   FAST

It's so popular, there's a written version of it at both my local drycleaner and my mechanic that says:

"We offer 3 kinds of services: good, cheap, fast. But you can only pick two. Good and cheap won't be fast. Fast and good won't be cheap. Cheap and fast won't be good."

What the model does is simplify something complex to only three trade-offs: time, quality, and cost. Of course, that's not the whole picture. What about employee wellbeing or environmental impact? What about customer experience or convenience? The model leaves those out. And that's the point. Every model includes some things and excludes others. That's what makes it a frame.

When I share a visual model with a group, I'll often say: "This model is not the truth, but truth can emerge from the model." Used well, models focus our attention and show us how big ideas fit together. Used poorly, they limit our thinking and create a false sense of certainty. Like all framing devices, we need to use them with care.

Change the space – the place frame

All the other framing devices focus on our words, but this one is about where those words are spoken. Physical locations have a subtle but significant impact on how we think, feel, and act. They can profoundly influence The Question Effect.

The seating controls the meeting

Winston Churchill once famously said, "We shape our buildings; thereafter they shape us." He was speaking about the architecture of the House of Commons, but the principle applies in every room. In fact, our brain contains specialised cells that ensure we understand the geometry and arrangement of the spaces we inhabit.

It's why my first action when leading a workshop or meeting is often to re-arrange the furniture. The seating will dictate the meeting:

- A boardroom setup encourages status updates, with one person talking at a time.
- Desks facing a screen says, "sit down and listen".
- Chairs in a circle says heart-to-heart dialogue.
- Small tables mean collaboration.
- Rows of chairs facing a stage screams lecture.

None of these setups is better than any other, but each supports a different kind of conversation.

This idea isn't new. We've known for centuries that spaces change our behaviour. Feng shui is the ancient Chinese practice of arranging living spaces to balance the flow of energy in a space. The Hogan in Navajo Culture in Southwestern United States is a circular dwelling that's considered a living, breathing entity that nurtures and protects its inhabitants. And there's the Māori practice of carved whare (meeting houses) that represent the body and spirit of an ancestor.

However, many of my clients act as if the furniture in their offices is bolted down. People give me shocked looks when I move a table. It's not until a workshop ends that people appreciate how much a change in furniture can change the quality of the conversation.

The land holds memory

Place is not just about rooms, but lands too. What is the history of a place? What happened here before? The ground beneath our feet holds stories that can deepen the quality of our conversations — if we take the time to acknowledge them.

In Māori culture, this is embedded in the mihimihi, a personal introduction that connects us to land that holds meaning for us. It's a way to share where we're from and how this has shaped us. I love hearing people's mihimihi because a shared place is such a fast way to build trust and understanding.

When I'm invited to a new place to run a leadership retreat, I'll always try to find out about the history of the land. What has happened here before? Who is connected to the land? What stories or tensions are still present? We can then use this knowledge to deepen the quality of our conversation. It's why the locations for UN climate conferences have increasingly been used to make symbolic statements. With Glasgow in 2021, the organisers chose a city with an industrial past that was transforming toward sustainability. The 2023 gathering in Dubai created tension precisely because of the geographical contradiction, with a climate conference hosted in a fossil fuel-dependent economy. This influenced both the negotiations and the public's perception of those negotiations.

In short, *where* we are changes *who* we are.

Choose the right frame

It's okay if you're feeling a bit overwhelmed by all the framing devices in this chapter. You don't need to remember them all. If you've got an important leadership challenge that needs to be well framed, you can use a tool I developed called The Framing Canvas. This helps you to choose the most useful framing device or devices for your unique leadership challenge.

You can access a printable version of The Framing Canvas as part of The Question Effect Toolkit at **www.paulmcgregor. co.nz/question-effect-toolkit.**

CHAPTER 13

Sensing

Reading the room

*"Humans don't communicate.
We miscommunicate
— and then clarify
the miscommunication."*

– Andrew O'Keeffe

t was the kind of workshop where something just felt off. I had been asked to facilitate an offsite for a team that hadn't met in person for years. They were stretched thin and finding time for a day away from the office was a real challenge.

On paper, it seemed straightforward. The leader described it as "lifting trust from a 7 to a 9". But after a few pre–session interviews, it was clear this wasn't a light tune-up. There were deeper rifts within the team, particularly between two team members.

I suggested postponing the group workshop but the manager reassured me, "People are just being dramatic." I agreed to go ahead, against my better judgment.

The morning was light and polite. We talked about ways of working and where things might improve. But over lunch, several people told me they thought we were skirting around the *real* issues.

So, after lunch, I decided to bring the elephant into the room. I invited them into a process to share honestly about what was challenging them at work.

To their credit, the group soon got the hang of it. A few people opened up with thoughtfulness and honesty, and the group responded warmly. Encouraged, I left the door open and kept asking: "Would anyone else like to share?"

In the space of thirty seconds, the conversation exploded. Years of frustration, anger, and grief came pouring out in one sharp, uncontrolled moment. It was loud, raw, and deeply painful. The room fell silent.

And just like that, we were in damage control.

The risk of ignoring

In the aftermath, I replayed things with mentors and family members — anyone who'd listen, really. The same thought kept coming back: *I knew this might happen.* I saw the signs. I felt them. But I didn't trust myself enough to act on them.

Good questions aren't enough. A curious attitude isn't enough. Even a well-designed process won't save us. As leaders, we need to read the room and be willing to move things forward or slow things down based on what we notice.

Questions can be weapons when it's unwise or unsafe to ask.

I might have had the right question that day, but I asked it at the wrong time, in the wrong way, to people who weren't ready for that level of honesty. The experience taught me that questions can be weapons when it's unwise or unsafe to ask. In this chapter, we'll explore how to develop this crucial sensing ability — your internal GPS for knowing when to ask, when to wait, and when people need something completely different. We'll unpack the three layers of sensing that can transform how you read any room, and discover practical ways to tune into the signals that most leaders miss entirely.

Why sensing matters

Reading the room has a real impact on team performance and engagement. Leaders who can quickly sense the temperature of the room are better able to respond and make smart decisions. But many of us are only scratching the surface of our sensing capabilities.

Let me illustrate this by asking a simple question: How many senses do you have? It shouldn't take you long to count to five: Taste. Touch. Hearing. Sight. Smell.

Easy, right?

But it's a trick question. The truth is, we have dozens of senses. Scientists still argue about how to classify them but most agree there are over 30. The idea of "the five senses" dates to Aristotle and has persisted only because of its simplicity.

How can we tell a plane is leaning over when our eyes are closed and music is blasting in our headphones? How do we know when to go to the toilet? When somebody is looking at us from the other side of the room? When our heart is beating faster? How can we feel itches on our skin? Feel pain inside our body? And what about when we have a gut instinct? Our gut is often called a second brain, as it communicates with our brain and influences our feelings and decisions.

These are just a few of the many senses scientists now recognise. Far too often, we ignore or distrust the signals our senses give us because we don't understand them.

The challenge is learning to trust what we can't fully explain. In our data-driven, evidence-hungry world,

The conscious mind can only process a tiny 0.0005% of all the data entering our brain.

these senses can feel unreliable. But research shows that our unconscious mind processes information far more quickly and comprehensively than our conscious mind. In fact, the human body sends 11 million bits per second to the brain for processing. However, the conscious mind can only process about 50 bits per second. That's a tiny 0.0005% of all the data entering our brain.

Most of this data is irrelevant. It's like when we're walking down a busy street, passing hundreds of people without a thought. Then, suddenly, we spot an old friend and — ping! — we light up. That's what sensing is. Our unconscious mind picks up on what matters, if we've trained it to notice.

The cost of missing these signals is enormous. Like I did in that doomed workshop, we might ask the wrong question at the wrong time — closing down possibilities rather than opening them up.

The three layers of sensing

To develop this sensing ability, I've found it helpful to think about three interconnected layers of awareness: observing, feeling, and intuiting. Tapping into all three layers gives us a much richer pool of data on which to base our decisions.

Layer 1: Observing — What our eyes and ears tell us

The brain devotes more space to vision than to all the other senses combined. And when it comes to people, we can often form surprisingly accurate judgments with very little information. Ambady and Rosenthal's famous "thin-slicing" research found that just 30 seconds of silent video can predict student ratings of teachers with remarkable accuracy.

But don't get too cocky. We're not always as good at reading body language as we might think, especially in new situations. Another psychological study, led by Bond and DePaulo, found that we're only 54% accurate at spotting lies from nonverbal cues. That's basically a coin toss. The meaning of body language also changes depending on the context. Folded arms might indicate defensiveness, or it could be a personal or cultural preference.

Mark Bowden, an expert in body language, says our brain is hardwired to presume the worst. When we see someone yawn during a presentation, our brain assumes they're bored. (But maybe they're just sleep-deprived?) When someone frowns, we assume they disagree. (Maybe that's just their resting face?) In the face of insufficient data, we jump to the worst conclusion because that's more likely to keep us safe. This was useful in the wild, but it's extremely unhelpful in our modern workplaces.

It's even harder now with virtual meetings (where we only have facial cues) and chat apps (where we only have emojis, if they are culturally acceptable).

So, what can we do instead?

Bowden suggests adding one word to any interpretation: *"maybe"*. The word reflects the statistical reality: our read could be wrong.

> "She looks frustrated... maybe."
> "They seem disengaged... maybe."
> "Those two are having an affair... maybe."

When we notice something, we can also try questioning it gently. One of my mentors, Matt Church, was brilliant at this:

- "Your voice went up at the end — are you doubting yourself?"
- "You were shaking your head as you said that — what's going on there?"
- "You lit up when you talked about that — did you feel that too?"

The key is to remain open-minded about whether our

assumptions are correct. Our observations are just one source of data.

Curious Questions: Set 13A

Before we hurry onwards, let's look at what you observe:

- What do you see as the biggest value of being able to read the room?
- What are the biggest barriers to reading the room in your workplace?
- How might you overcome those?

adapted from the work of Gloria Wilcox

Layer 2: Feeling — Our emotional compass

We touched on this in *The Conflict Question*, but it bears repeating: emotions are data that influence behaviour. When we take control of that data, we can control how we respond. The alternative is that our emotions take over.

Many of us presume that we respond to events as they happen. In truth, we respond to the emotion that the event triggers. For instance, we don't yell at somebody because they haven't done as we've asked; we yell at them because we *feel* frustration and anger.

The problem I found with this years ago was that I had no way of describing or understanding my emotions. How could I expect to master my response to the emotions if I couldn't even identify them? Good, sad, happy, disappointed, and frustrated were probably the extent of my vocabulary. Tui Williams, a relationships coach, introduced me to *The Feeling Wheel*, a tool developed by Gloria Wilcox. I printed it out and stuck it on my wall. It gave me the vocabulary to decode the messages my emotions were trying to tell me.

This skill is called emotional granularity and the research on this has found that people who can differentiate their emotions are much better at recovering from setbacks and making constructive decisions. This makes sense when you think about it; they're not controlled by the emotion but can choose their response.

For instance, anger is our body's way of communicating

"no." It tells us a boundary has been crossed. Tui taught me the difference between *feeling anger* (noticing it, naming it, staying in control) and *being angry* (getting swept up in it, reacting without choice).

Becoming emotionally literate may sound a bit woo-woo, but it's a foundational leadership capability. The more we listen to our bodies, the more we learn – and the better we're able to respond when tensions arise.

Layer 3: Intuiting — Rapid pattern recognition

I see intuition as the integration of every signal we receive: what we've observed, what we've felt, and what our unconscious brain has quietly been piecing together. Herbert Simon describes it as "recognition of familiar patterns" — a rapid, unconscious matching of what's happening with past experiences. In other words, intuition is pre-rational. Remember, we become consciously aware of only 0.0005% of all the information our brain processes. Intuition is pattern recognition before the pattern becomes obvious.

> Intuition is pattern recognition before the pattern becomes obvious.

The challenge is holding our intuitions lightly. They are precious, but not perfect. Daniel Kahneman (a sceptic of intuition) suggests that we should trust it only in situations that we've experienced before. If we have no prior experiences on which to base our supposed intuition, is it really intuition at all?

Like observations and feelings, our intuitions are to be taken as one data source amongst many. We must notice them and then validate them with — you guessed it — questions.

But of course, even when we know all this, we can still get it wrong.

> **Curious Questions: Set 13B**
>
> For our final set of curious questions, let's turn inward:
>
> - How aware are you of how different emotions show up in your body?
> - What emotions do you find challenging to experience yourself?
> - What emotions do you find most challenging to respond to?
> - When do you think you *can* trust your intuition?

Still practising

I've often replayed that doomed workshop in my mind. Why did I ignore the signals? What could I have done differently? I knew something was off, and I didn't trust my own knowing. I listened to the manager, but not to myself.

Sensing is a practice of being present. It's about paying attention, and then having the courage to act on what we notice.

If I had my time again in that workshop, I would have dialled back the expectations and slowed down the process. Put simply, I would have checked the group before turning up the heat.

The best leaders I know don't simply charge ahead with confidence. They pause, notice, and stay humble when things change. They know when to move forward, when to pull back, and when to wait in the silence just a little longer.

Good questions don't work in the wrong conditions. Sensing helps us choose *when* to ask, *how* to ask, and *whether* to ask at all. That's what I'm still learning to do. And I hope, as you finish this chapter, it's something you'll practise too.

CHAPTER 14

An invitation

Always be asking

"Ring the bells that can still ring, forget your perfect offering. There is a crack, a crack in everything: that's how the light gets in."

– Leonard Cohen

Years ago, when my mentor asked me, "Do you want to learn this lesson here or in the next role?", I didn't anticipate what this would spark in me — from searching for answers to staying curious with bigger questions.

Since then, the world has changed dramatically.

Generative AI can now answer our questions faster than ever. At best, it promises to speed up mundane tasks and stretch human invention to a new level. But as the world rushes to adopt AI, I've been wondering: What sort of leadership do we need in this emerging partnership? What aspects of being human must we seek to retain? And what must we never delegate to the machines?

For all its capabilities, AI still can't hold silence. It can't sense the tension in a room or notice what's unsaid. It can't lead a group through an important conversation with empathy, timing, and care. Only humans can do that. And we do it best when we're curious. The Question Effect takes us to the heart of what matters, faster. Questions draw others in and open space for fresh insights to emerge, allowing us to adapt as the world changes.

We don't need to be perfect leaders with all the answers. As Leonard Cohen reminds us, it's often through the cracks that the light gets in. The Question Effect opens those cracks and lets in insights, perspectives, and possibilities.

If you remember just one thing from this book, let it be this: Leadership isn't about having the right answers, but about asking better questions. Throughout history, the most positive leaders have been those who have helped us to dig deeper under the surface to question unspoken assumptions — and move forward from a place of curiosity and care.

We need more of those bigger, bolder conversations right now — and with The Question Effect, you can be the catalyst.

Acknowledgements

Writing this book has been the most challenging project I've ever undertaken. Self–doubt threatened to destroy the project on multiple occasions, including when I axed 30,000 words from an early manuscript and started afresh with a new concept. Or what about the sheer number of hours invested at 5am or 7pm when I could have been doing other things? Sleep? TV? Relaxation? Who needs those, right?

Thank you to Chris and Elise for that comedy-of-errors writing trip in your camper. That got me going again when I had lost faith in this project.

Thank you to all my clients and readers who shared encouragement and critique.

Thank you to Matt Church for encouraging me to play a bigger game — and for breaking down the process piece-by-piece.

Thank you to my fellow Thought Leaders Business School alumni, especially Josh Comrie, Hester van der Spiegel, Michael Watts, Simi Rayat, Trudy Graham, Jo Clancy, and Matthew Needham. Having a crew who 'get it' means so much to me.

Thank you to all the team at Hambone Publishing. Writing

the book was hard enough; you made all the other logistical parts so much easier, not to mention providing much needed boosts of confidence when I was flagging.

But the biggest thank you goes to my family, and especially to you Ellie. You put up with countless lonely nights and coffee-deprived mornings while I beavered away in the back bedroom. You never doubted me. Thank you for allowing me the space to explore and grow.

Connect with me

I'm obsessed with how humans interact and create impact. I love working with leaders and teams who want to make more progress, faster, but feel overloaded, overwhelmed, or quite simply over it. To inquire about leadership programmes, mentoring, keynotes, or MCing, please visit **paulmcgregor.co.nz**.

And if you found this book valuable, I'd love to hear from you by email at **paul@paulmcgregor.co.nz**.

References

Chapter 1 – A fundamental shift

Asana. (2023). Anatomy of work index. Asana. https://asana.com/resources/anatomy-of-work

Jung, C. G. (1959). The Archetypes and the Collective Unconscious (Collected Works Vol. 9, Part 1). Princeton, NJ: Princeton University Press. (Original work published 1959.)

Chapter 2 – Complexity demands curiosity

Azhar, A. (2025, April 9). How to win as the world changes (Exponential View newsletter). https://www.exponentialview.co/p/how-to-win-as-the-world-changes

Brehm, J. W. (1966). A theory of psychological reactance. Academic Press.

Gallup, Inc. (2025). State of the Global Workplace: 2025 Report. Washington, DC: Gallup Press. https://www.gallup.com/workplace/349484/state-of-the-global-workplace.aspx

Harter, J. K., Schmidt, F. L., Agrawal, S., & Plowman, S. K. (2013). The relationship between engagement at work and organizational outcomes: 2012 Q12 meta-analysis. Gallup, Inc.

Skonord, C. (2024, August 3). The success of Toyota's employee suggestion program. Ideawake. https://ideawake.com/the-success-of-toyotas-employee-suggestion-program/

Chapter 3 – The question cliff

Berger, W. (2014). A More Beautiful Question: The Power of Inquiry to Spark Breakthrough Ideas. New York: Bloomsbury.

Best Practice Institute. (2019, October 2). Have the courage to ask. Best Practice Institute. https://blog.bestpracticeinstitute.org/have-the-courage-to-ask/

Engelmann, J. B., Meyer, F., Ruff, C. C., & Schlicht, E. J. (2019). The social transmission of information-seeking behavior in human groups. Psychological Science, 30(12), 1876–1886. https://doi.org/10.1177/0956797619878825

Gruber, M. J., Gelman, B. D., & Ranganath, C. (2014). States of curiosity modulate hippocampus-dependent learning via the dopaminergic circuit. Neuron, 84(2), 486–496. https://doi.org/10.1016/j.neuron.2014.08.060

Haidt, J. (2006). The happiness hypothesis: Finding modern truth in ancient wisdom. Basic Books.

Hatfield, E., Cacioppo, J. T., & Rapson, R. L. (1994). Emotional contagion. Cambridge University Press.

Heintz, S., & Ruch, W. (2022). Cross-sectional age differences in 24 character strengths: Five meta-analyses from early adolescence to late adulthood. The Journal of Positive Psychology, 17(3), 356–374. https://doi.org/10.1080/17439760.2021.1871938

Huang, K., Yeomans, M., Brooks, A., Minson, J., & Gino, F. (2017). It doesn't hurt to ask: Question-asking increases liking. Journal of Personality and Social Psychology, 113(3), 430–452.

Kamprad, I., & Torekull, B. (1999). Leading by design: The IKEA story. Harper Business.

Kashdan, T. B., & Silvia, P. J. (2009). Curiosity and interest: The benefits of thriving on novelty and challenge. In S. J. Lopez & C. R. Snyder (Eds.), Oxford handbook of positive psychology (2nd ed., pp. 367–374). Oxford University Press.

Kashdan, T. B. (2025, September 22). Everything you wanted to know about curiosity but didn't ask. Provoked with Dr. Todd Kashdan. https://toddkashdan.substack.com/p/everything-you-wanted-on-curiosity toddkashdan.substack.com+1

Kashdan, T. B. (2022, October 12). Correcting a misunderstanding about curiosity. Provoked with Dr. Todd Kashdan. https://toddkashdan.substack.com/p/correcting-a-misunderstanding-about

Litman, J. A. (2005). Curiosity and the pleasures of learning: Wanting and liking new information. Cognition & Emotion, 19(6), 793–814. https://doi.org/10.1080/02699930541000102

Lydon-Staley, D. M., Perry-Zurn, M., & Bassett, D. S. (2020). Within-person variability in curiosity during daily life and implications for well-being. Social Cognitive and Affective Neuroscience, 16(3), 215–224.

Norton, M. I., Mochon, D., & Ariely, D. (2012). The "IKEA effect": When labor leads to love. Journal of Consumer Psychology, 22(3), 453–460.

Schwaba, T., Luhmann, M., Denissen, J. J. A., Chung, J. M., & Bleidorn, W. (2018). Openness to experience and culture–openness transactions across the lifespan. Journal of Personality and Social Psychology, 115(1), 118–136. https://doi.org/10.1037/pspp0000150

Twenge, J. M. (2019, March 19). Teens increasingly disconnected from books, TV, movies. San Diego State University – Department of Psychology. https://psychology.sdsu.edu/teens-increasingly-disconnected-from-books-tv-

Chapter 4 – Seven leadership challenges

Drucker, P. F. (as cited in Bryant, A.). (2012, September 11). How to consult like Peter Drucker. Forbes. https://www.forbes.com/sites/drucker/2012/09/11/how-to-consult-like-peter-drucker/

Chapter 5 – The Vision Question

Asana. (2023). Anatomy of work index. Asana. https://asana.com/resources/anatomy-of-work

Carver, G. W. (n.d.). Where there is no vision, there is no hope. [Quote attributed]. Retrieved August 22, 2025, from https://www.goodreads.com/author/quotes/15619.George_Washington_Carver

Senge, P. M. (1990). The Fifth Discipline: The Art and Practice of the Learning Organization. New York: Doubleday.

Skonord, C. (2024, August 3). The success of Toyota's employee suggestion program. Ideawake. https://ideawake.com/the-success-of-toyotas-employee-suggestion-program/

Te Kāiā te Rangatira. (n.d.). Miriana Stephens. Retrieved August 22, 2025, from https://www.tekaiaterangatira.com/speakers/show/14-Miriana%20Stephens

Te Tauihu Intergenerational Strategy. (2022). Te Tauihu Intergenerational Strategy. Wakatū Incorporation. https://www.tetauihu.nz/

Chapter 6 – The Strategy Question

Bohns, V. K., Roghanizad, M. M., & Xu, A. Z. (2014). Underestimating our influence over others' unethical behavior and decisions. Personality and Social Psychology Bulletin, 40(3), 348–362. https://doi.org/10.1177/0146167213511825

Business Lab. (2020, December 22). Ep 8: On Strategy, With Alicia McKay [Audio podcast episode]. In Beyond Consultation. Business Lab. https://www.businesslab.co.nz/beyond-consultation-podcast/8

Business Lab. (2022). St John: Creating a strategy that works in practice [Case study]. Business Lab. https://www.business-lab.co.nz/results/stjohnstrategy

Fake, C. (2009, Sept. 28). "Working Hard Is Overrated." Business Insider. (Reprinted from Caterina.net) https://www.businessinsider.com/working-hard-is-overrated-2009-9#:~:text=thousands%20of%20materials%20looking%20for,more%20important%20than%20working%20hard.

Goodhart, C. A. E. (1975). Problems of Monetary Management: The U.K. Experience. Papers in Monetary Economics (Reserve Bank of Australia).

Robertson, D. A., & Breen, B. (2013). Brick by Brick: How LEGO Rewrote the Rules of Innovation and Conquered the Toy Industry. Crown Business.

Rumelt, R. P. (2011). Good Strategy/Bad Strategy: The Difference and Why It Matters. New York: Crown Publishing.

Smith, A. M. (2024, July 17). The strategy secret of LEGO [Post]. LinkedIn. https://www.linkedin.com/posts/alex-m-h-smith_the-strategy-secret-of-lego-activity-7213865884191207424-_MLT/

Ury, W. (2007). The power of a positive no: How to say no and still get to yes. Bantam Books.

Wilson, R. C., Geana, A., White, J. M., Ludvig, E. A., & Cohen, J. D. (2014). Humans use directed and random exploration to solve the explore–exploit dilemma. Journal of Experimental Psychology: General, 143(6), 2074–2081. https://doi.org/10.1037/a0038199

Chapter 7 – The Culture Question

Adler, S., Campion, M., Colquitt, A., Grubb, A., Murphy, K., Ollander-Krechel, L., ... Pulakos, E. (2016). Getting rid of performance ratings: Genius or folly? *Industrial and Organizational Psychology, 9*(2), 219–252. https://doi.org/10.1017/iop.2016.9

Edmondson, A. C. (1999). Psychological safety and learning behavior in work teams. *Administrative Science Quarterly, 44*(2), 350–383.

Gallup, Inc. (2025). *State of the Global Workplace: 2025 Report.* Washington, DC: Gallup Press. https://www.gallup.com/workplace/349484/state-of-the-global-workplace.aspx

Google. (2015). *Guide: Understand team effectiveness* (Project Aristotle). re:Work. https://rework.withgoogle.com/guides/understanding-team-effectiveness/

Kashdan, T. B. (2021). *The art of insubordination: How to dissent and defy effectively.* Avery.

Kluger, A. N., & DeNisi, A. (1996). The effects of feedback interventions on performance: A historical review, a meta-analysis, and a preliminary feedback intervention theory. *Psychological Bulletin, 119*(2), 254–284. https://doi.org/10.1037/0033-2909.119.2.254

Schwartz, T., Gomes, J., & McCarthy, C. (2010). *The way we're working isn't working: The four forgotten needs that energize great performance.* Free Press.

Sull, D., Sull, C., & Zweig, B. (2022). Toxic culture is driving the Great Resignation. *MIT Sloan Management Review, 63*(2).

Wilson, M. (2023). *Shift: Everyday Actions Leaders Can Take to Shift Culture.* [Self-published].

Chapter 8 – The Perspectives Question

Bertrand, M., & Mullainathan, S. (2004). Are Emily and Greg more employable than Lakisha and Jamal? *American Economic Review, 94*(4), 991–1013. https://doi.org/10.1257/0002828042002561

Bose, D., Segui-Gomez, M., & Crandall, J. R. (2011). Vulnerability of female drivers involved in motor vehicle crashes: An analysis of US population at risk. *American Journal of Public Health, 101*(12), 2368–2373. https://doi.org/10.2105/AJPH.2011.300275

Bowden, M. (Guest), & Hughes, L. (Host). (2022, June 27). *World-leading body language expert Mark Bowden talks facilitation* [Audio podcast episode]. In *First Time Facilitator*. Leanne Hughes. https://podcast.leannehughes.com/videos/world-leading-body-language-expert-mark-bowden-talks-facilitation-on-leanne-hughes-podcast/

Buolamwini, J., & Gebru, T. (2018). Gender shades: Intersectional accuracy disparities in commercial gender classification. In S. A. Friedler & C. Wilson (Eds.), *Proceedings of Machine Learning Research: Vol. 81*. Conference on Fairness, Accountability and Transparency (pp. 1–15). PMLR.

Business Lab. (2020, September 14). *Where next for community engagement?* Business Lab. https://www.businesslab.co.nz/insights/where-next-for-community-engagement

Greenwald, A. G., McGhee, D. E., & Schwartz, J. L. K. (1998). Measuring individual differences in implicit cognition: The Implicit Association Test. *Journal of Personality and Social Psychology, 74*(6), 1464–1480. https://doi.org/10.1037/0022-3514.74.6.1464

Greenwald, A. G., Nosek, B. A., & Banaji, M. R. (2003). Understanding and using the Implicit Association Test: II. Method variables and construct validity. *Journal of Personality and Social Psychology, 85*(2), 197–216. https://doi.org/10.1037/0022-3514.85.2.197

Hoffman, K. M., Trawalter, S., Axt, J. R., & Oliver, M. N. (2016). Racial bias in pain assessment and treatment recommendations, and false beliefs about biological differences. *Proceedings of the National Academy of Sciences, 113*(16), 4296–4301. https://doi.org/10.1073/pnas.1516047113

Hunt, V., Layton, D., & Prince, S. (2015). *Diversity matters.* McKinsey & Company. https://www.mckinsey.com/~/media/mckinsey/business%20functions/organization/our%20insights/why%20diversity%20matters/diversity%20matters.pdf

Judge, T. A., & Cable, D. M. (2004). The effect of physical height on workplace success and income: Preliminary test of a theoretical model. *Journal of Applied Psychology, 89*(3), 428–441. https://doi.org/10.1037/0021-9010.89.3.428

Lazzaro, S. (2017, August 21). Is this soap dispenser racist? *The New Zealand Herald.* https://www.nzherald.co.nz/world/is-this-soap-dispenser-racist-controversy-as-video-of-machine-that-only-responds-to-white-skin/67MHYDYYNABX-4NIYO2OBUN4RV4/

Lorde, A. (1984). *Sister outsider: Essays and speeches.* Crossing Press.

Ministry of Justice. (n.d.). *National action plan against racism.* New Zealand Government. Retrieved August 28, 2025, from https://www.justice.govt.nz/justice-sector-policy/key-initiatives/national-action-plan-against-racism/

Mustard, D. B. (2001). Racial, ethnic, and gender disparities in sentencing: Evidence from the U.S. federal courts. *Journal of Law and Economics, 44*(1), 285–314. https://doi.org/10.1086/320276

Myers, V. (2012). *Moving diversity forward: How to go from well-meaning to well-doing.* American Bar Association.

NextGen Engagement. (n.d.). *NextGen Engagement: Advancing the practice of engagement for the next generation.* Retrieved August 28, 2025, from https://www.nextgenengagement.org/

Nørretranders, T. (1998). *The user illusion: Cutting consciousness down to size*. Penguin Books.

Perez, C. C. (2019). *Invisible women: Data bias in a world designed for men*. Abrams Press.

Project Implicit. (n.d.). *Take a test*. Harvard University. Retrieved August 27, 2025, from https://app-prod-03.implicit.harvard.edu/implicit/demo/

Silverman, S. (2018, January 5). Twitter thread responding to online harassment [Social media post]. Twitter. (Covered in Gibson, C., *Washington Post*, Jan 5, 2018).

Tajfel, H., & Turner, J. C. (1979). An integrative theory of intergroup conflict. In W. G. Austin & S. Worchel (Eds.), *The social psychology of intergroup relations* (pp. 33–47). Brooks/Cole.

Wikipedia contributors. (2025, February 21). *List of cognitive biases*. In *Wikipedia*. https://en.wikipedia.org/wiki/List_of_cognitive_biases

Chapter 9 – The Experience Question

American Customer Satisfaction Index. (n.d.). *The American Customer Satisfaction Index*. Retrieved August 28, 2025, from https://theacsi.org/

Angelou, M. (n.d.). "I've learned that people will forget what you said, people will forget what you did, but people will never forget how you made them feel." [Quote attributed]. Source not verified.

Epley, N., & Schroeder, J. (2014). Mistakenly seeking solitude. *Journal of Experimental Psychology: General, 143*(5), 1980–1999. https://doi.org/10.1037/a0037323

Fornell, C., Morgeson, F. V., III, Hult, G. T. M., & VanAmburg, D. (2020). *The reign of the customer: Customer-centric approaches to improving satisfaction*. Palgrave Macmillan.

Haar, J. (2024, May 3). *Job insecurity drives Aotearoa New Zealand workforce to highest burnout risk*. Massey University News.

Kahneman, D. (2011). *Thinking, Fast and Slow*. New York: Farrar, Straus and Giroux.

Kahneman, D., Fredrickson, B. L., Schreiber, C. A., & Redelmeier, D. A. (1993). When more pain is preferred to less: Adding a better end. *Psychological Science, 4*(6), 401–405. https://doi.org/10.1111/j.1467-9280.1993.tb00589

Taylor, M. (2022, November 11). *Why Les Schwab runs to your car*. Strixus Leadership Journal. https://strixus.com/entry/why-les-schwab-runs-to-your-car-17808

Van Kleef, G. A. (2009). How emotions regulate social life: The emotions as social information (EASI) model. *Current Directions in Psychological Science, 18*(3), 184–188. https://doi.org/10.1111/j.1467-8721.2009.01633

Van Kleef, G. A. (2016). *The interpersonal dynamics of emotion: Toward an integrative theory of emotions as social information*. Cambridge University Press.

Chapter 10 – The Conflict Question

Gandhi, M. K. (n.d.). "Peace is not the absence of conflict, but the ability to cope with it." [Quote attributed]. Source not verified.

Hurt, K., & Dye, D. (2023). *World Workplace Conflict and Collaboration Survey*. Let's Grow Leaders (White Paper).

Chapter 11 – The Learning Question

Business Lab (Producer). (2021, October 6). *Ep 29 – Human Learning Systems for Aotearoa New Zealand (with Dr. Toby Lowe)* [Audio podcast episode]. In *Beyond Consultation*. Business Lab. https://www.businesslab.co.nz/beyond-consultation-podcast/29

Cameron, W. B. (1963). *Informal Sociology: A Casual Introduction to Sociological Thinking*. New York: Random House.

Hoffman, R. (2023, September 8). "You are Generation AI" (Commencement address). Bologna Business School, University of Bologna. [Transcript available on ReidHoffman.org].

Lifehack. (2017). *2013–2017 Final Impact Report*. Enspiral. https://lifehackhq.co/lifehack-resources/2013-2017-final-impact-report/

Lowe, T. et al. (2020). *Human Learning Systems: Public Service for the Real World*. London: RSA.

Lowe, T. (2023, November 28). How measuring impact gets in the way of real world change. *Integration and Implementation Insights*. https://i2insights.org/2023/11/28/measuring-impact-is-counterproductive/

McGregor, P. (Host). (2023, October 25). *Ep 71: A human, learning systems approach to The Construction Accord, with Judy Zhang* [Audio podcast episode]. In *Beyond Consultation*. Apple Podcasts. https://podcasts.apple.com/nz/podcast/ep-71-a-human-learning-systems-approach-to/id1501598908?i=1000631941740

Chapter 12 – Framing

Fairhurst, G. T. (2011). *The Power of Framing: Creating the Language of Leadership*. San Francisco: Jossey-Bass.

Hooton, M. (2023, February 23). It's too late to avoid climate change—now we have to adapt [Opinion]. *The New Zealand Herald*.

IMDb. (n.d.). *Philadelphia (1993) – Quotes*. IMDb. Retrieved August 28, 2025, from https://www.imdb.com/title/tt0107818/quotes/

Lakoff, G. (2004). *Don't Think of an Elephant!: Know Your Values and Frame the Debate*. White River Junction, VT: Chelsea Green Publishing.

Mazzucato, M. (2016, Dec 24). Interview: "The failures of capitalism have led to Brexit and a Donald Trump presidency." *Salon.com* (interview by L. S. Parramore). https://www.salon.com/2016/12/24/the-failures-of-capitalism-have-lead-to-brexit-and-a-trump-presidency_partner/#:~:text=They%20focused%20on%20a%20supposed,problems%20leads%20to%20simplistic%20answers.

Mortland, C. (2023, February 24). When your plumbing springs a leak … [Post]. LinkedIn. https://www.linkedin.com/posts/carolyn-mortland-08b381_matthew-hooton-its-too-late-to-avoid-climate-activity-7034599497703858176-q2DU/?originalSubdomain=nz

Siegel, D. J. (2010). *The mindful therapist: A clinician's guide to mindsight and neural integration*. W. W. Norton & Company.

Simmons, J. P., & Nelson, L. D. (2013, December 19). "Exactly": The Most Famous Framing Effect Is Robust To Precise Wording [Blog post]. *Data Colada*. https://datacolada.org/11

Tajfel, H., & Turner, J. C. (1979). An integrative theory of intergroup conflict. In W. G. Austin & S. Worchel (Eds.), *The social psychology of intergroup relations* (pp. 33–47). Brooks/Cole.

Tversky, A., & Kahneman, D. (1981). The framing of decisions and the psychology of choice. *Science, 211*(4481), 453–458.

Chapter 13 – Reading the room

Ambady, N., & Rosenthal, R. (1992). Thin slices of expressive behavior as predictors of interpersonal consequences: A meta-analysis. *Psychological Bulletin, 111*(2), 256–274. https://doi.org/10.1037/0033-2909.111.2.256

Bond, C. F., Jr., & DePaulo, B. M. (2006). Accuracy of deception judgments. *Personality and Social Psychology Review, 10*(3), 214–4. https://doi.org/10.1207/s15327957pspr1003_223

Kahneman, D., & Klein, G. (2009). Conditions for intuitive expertise: A failure to disagree. *American Psychologist, 64*(6), 515–526. https://doi.org/10.1037/a0016755

McGregor, P. (Host). (2022, January 31). *Ep 37: How to Harness the Science of Human Instincts, with Andrew O'Keeffe* [Audio podcast episode]. In *Beyond Consultation*. Business Lab. https://www.businesslab.co.nz/beyond-consultation-podcast/37

O'Keeffe, A. (2011). *Hardwired Humans: Successful Leadership Using Human Instincts*. Sydney: Roundtable Press.

Simon, H. A. (1987). Making management decisions: The role of intuition and emotion. *The Academy of Management Executive, 1*(1), 57–64.

Watts, D. J. (2011). *Everything Is Obvious (Once You Know the Answer)*. New York: Crown Business.

Willcox, G. (1982). The feeling wheel: A tool for expanding awareness of emotions and increasing spontaneity and intimacy. *Transactional Analysis Journal, 12*(4), 274–276.

Wilson, T. D. (2002). *Strangers to ourselves: Discovering the adaptive unconscious*. Harvard University Press.

Young, E. (2021). *Super senses: The science of your 32 senses and how to use them*. John Murray.

Chapter 14 – An invitation

Cohen, L. (1992). "Anthem." On *The Future* [Album]. Columbia Records.

Recommended Reading

1. Leadership and Strategy

Edmondson, A. C. (2018). *The fearless organization: Creating psychological safety in the workplace for learning, innovation, and growth*. Wiley.

Heath, D. (2020). *Upstream: The quest to solve problems before they happen*. Avid Reader Press.

Kahneman, D. (2011). *Thinking, fast and slow*. Farrar, Straus and Giroux.

Mintzberg, H., Ahlstrand, B. W., & Lampel, J. (2005). *Strategy bites back: It is a lot more, and less, than you ever imagined*. Pearson Education.

Rumelt, R. P. (2011). *Good strategy/bad strategy: The difference and why it matters*. Crown Business.

Scott, K. (2017). *Radical candor: Be a kick-ass boss without losing your humanity*. St. Martin's Press.

2. Facilitation and Change

Block, P. (2009). *Community: The structure of belonging*. Berrett-Koehler.

Cazaly, L. (2016). *Leader as facilitator: How to engage, inspire and get work done*. Melbourne Books.

Eastwood, O. (2021). *Belonging: The ancient code of togetherness*. Hachette.

Hunter, D. (2007). *The art of facilitation: The essentials for leading great meetings and creating group synergy*. Jossey-Bass.

Kahane, A. (2004). *Solving tough problems: An open way of talking, listening, and creating new realities*. Berrett-Koehler.

Kaner, S. (2014). *Facilitator's guide to participatory decision-making* (3rd ed.). Jossey-Bass.

Parker, P. (2018). *The art of gathering: How we meet and why it matters*. Riverhead Books.

Senge, P. M. (1990). *The fifth discipline: The art and practice of the learning organization*. Doubleday.

Wilson, M. (2023). *Shift: Everyday actions leaders can take to shift culture*. [Self-published].

3. Curiosity and Communication

Berger, W. (2014). *A more beautiful question: The power of inquiry to spark breakthrough ideas*. Bloomsbury.

Bungay Stanier, M. (2016). *The coaching habit: Say less, ask more & change the way you lead forever*. Box of Crayons Press.

Duhigg, C. (2023). *Supercommunicators: How to unlock the secret language of connection*. Random House.

Kashdan, T. B. (2009). *Curious?: Discover the missing ingredient to a fulfilling life*. HarperCollins.

Kashdan, T. B. (2021). *The art of insubordination: How to dissent and defy effectively*. Avery.

Kline, N. (1999). *Time to think: Listening to ignite the human mind*. Cassell.

O'Keeffe, A. (2011). *Hardwired humans: Our innate behaviors and how to manage them*. Finch Publishing.

Rouse, S. (2021). *Understanding body language: How to decode nonverbal communication in life, love, and work*. HarperOne.